TEACHING
literacy
IN THE digital AGE

Inspiration for all levels and literacies

EDITED BY MARK GL

D1361186

International Society for Technology in Education
EUGENE, OREGON • WASHINGTON, DC

Teaching Literacy in the Digital Age:
Inspiration for All Levels and Literacies
Edited by Mark Gura

© 2014 International Society for Technology in Education

Production Editor: *Lynda Gansel*
Production Coordinator: *Emily Reed*
Copy Editor: *Katherine Gries*
Proofreader: *Ann Skaugset*
Indexer: *Wendy Allex*
Cover Design: *Tamra Holmes*
Book Design and Production: *Kim McGovern*

Library of Congress Cataloging-in-Publication Data

Teaching literacy in the digital age: inspiration for all levels and
    literacies / edited by Mark Gura.
      pages cm
    Includes bibliographical references and index.
    ISBN 978-1-56484-339-5 (pbk.) — ISBN 978-1-56484-482-8 (e-book)
    1. Language arts—Computer-assisted instruction. 2. Language arts—
Computer network resources. 3. Language arts—Audio-visual aids.
    4. Computers and literacy. 5. Educational technology.   I. Gura, Mark.
    LB1576.7.T415 2014
    372.6'0440785—dc23
                                                    2013019201

First Edition
ISBN: 978-1-56484-339-5 (paperback)
ISBN: 978-1-56484-482-8 (e-book)

Printed in the United States of America

ISTE® is a registered trademark of the International Society for Technology in Education.

About ISTE

The International Society for Technology in Education is the premier membership association for educators and education leaders committed to empowering connected learners in a connected world. Home to the ISTE Conference and Expo and the widely adopted ISTE Standards for learning, teaching, and leading in the digital age, the association represents more than 100,000 professionals worldwide.

We support our members with professional development, networking opportunities, advocacy, and ed tech resources to help advance the transformation of education. To find out more about these and other ISTE initiatives, visit iste.org.

As part of our mission, ISTE works with experienced educators to develop and publish practical resources for classroom teachers, teacher educators and technology leaders. Every manuscript we select for publication is carefully peer reviewed and professionally edited.

Also by Mark Gura

Getting Started with LEGO Robotics: A Guide for K–12 Educators

Visual Arts Units for All Levels

Related ISTE Titles

Bookmapping: Lit Trips and Beyond
Terence W. Cavanaugh, Jerome Burg

Digital Storytelling Guide for Educators
Midge Frazel

English Language Arts Units for Grades 9–12
Christopher Shamburg

From Inspiration to Red Carpet: Host Your Own Student Film Festival
William L. Bass, Christian Goodrich, Kim Lindskog

Making Connections with Blogging: Authentic Learning for Today's Classrooms
Lisa Parisi, Brian Crosby

Serious Comix
Eydie Wilson

Student-Powered Podcasting: Teaching for 21st-Century Literacy
Christopher Shamburg

To see all books available from ISTE, please visit iste.org/bookstore

About the Editor

Mark Gura has been an educator for more than three decades. The former director of instructional technology of the New York City Department of Education, he began his career as a teacher, and spent 18 years in elementary and middle school classrooms in Harlem. More recently, he has taught graduate education courses at Fordham University, Touro College, and New York Institute of Technology. Gura was a staff and curriculum developer for NYC's Central Division of Curriculum and Instruction before being recruited to develop and administer the first citywide instructional technology program. He has written extensively on education for the *New York Daily News, Converge,* and a variety of other education magazines, and has written and published numerous books on education, including *Getting Started with LEGO Robotics* (ISTE, 2011), and *Visual Arts Units for All Levels* (ISTE, 2008). Gura currently runs SIGLIT, ISTE's literacy special interest group. He has been involved in professional development podcasting for educators for many years, and is the producer/host of ISTE's SIGLIT podcast "Literacy Special Interest."

Gura has spoken on the subject of instructional technology throughout the United States. He lives in Jupiter, Florida, teaching graduate teacher education courses online, as well as writing and podcasting there. Drawing on his work as a teacher, professional and curriculum specialist, and professor of graduate level teacher education courses, Gura developed and has broadly shared with classroom teacher colleagues the practice featured in Chapter 8, Graphic Novel: Style Writing Projects. The project combines his interest in visual arts education and literacy instruction. ISTE special interest group (SIG) affiliations: SIGLIT (literacy) and SIGAE (arts educators).

About the Contributors

L. Kay Abernathy is an associate professor and coordinator of Educational Technology Leadership, Lamar University in Beaumont, Texas. She holds an EdD in Educational Administration from Texas A&M University. She is an ISTE member, past board member of the Consortium for School Networking (CoSN), and past president of the Texas Computer Education Association. Her research interests include leadership in using Web 2.0 tools, online learning, reflective professional development, and a major project within the Inter/National Coalition for Electronic Portfolio Research. ISTE special interest group (SIG) affiliation: SIGLIT.

Sheryl R. Abshire, PhD, an assistant professor of educational leadership at Lamar University in Beaumont, Texas, is an active ISTE member, past chair and present board member for CoSN, past president of Louisiana Association of Computer Using Educators (LACUE), co-chair of the ISTE/CoSN Policy Committee, and serves on the Universal Service Administrative Company (USAC) board. As a former school principal, K–5 teacher, library/media specialist, and chief technology officer, her honors include ISTE Public Policy Advocate of the Year, 2012 Louisiana Governors E-Award, and 2013 NCTET Technology Community Builder award. Her research interests include online learning, leadership, technology, and e-portfolios. ISTE SIG affiliation: SIGLIT.

Gerald W. Aungst, a public school educator since 1991, is the supervisor of gifted and elementary mathematics for the school district of Cheltenham Township, Pennsylvania. He taught for 18 years at the elementary level, both as a classroom teacher and a gifted support specialist. Aungst is the author of *Recess At Last,* which placed fifteenth in the 14th Annual Interactive Fiction Competition, and is the webmaster and co-creator of All About Explorers (www.allaboutexplorers. com), a website for introducing elementary students to information literacy skills. ISTE SIG affiliations: SIGLIT, SIGAdmin, SIGDS (digital storytelling), SIGVE (virtual environments).

William L. Bass is a former middle and high school English teacher who now works with teachers as an instructional coach in the Parkway School District, St. Louis, Missouri, and as an adjunct professor for Missouri Baptist University. Bass holds a Master of Science in Instructional Technology and a Bachelor of Science in English. He is co-president of the Educational Technology Association of Greater St. Louis, a Google Certified Teacher, and a past member of the National Council of Teachers of English (NCTE) executive committee. He is the senior author of *From Inspiration to Red Carpet: Host Your Own Student Film Festival* (ISTE 2013). Bass is very active with ISTE SIGs. He is president-elect of ISTE's special interest group for innovative learning technologies (SIGILT). Other ISTE SIG affiliations: SIGLIT, SIGAdmin, SIGETC (educational technology coaches), SIGMS (media specialists), SIGOL (online learning), SIGTE (teacher educators), and SIGTC (technology coordinators).

Angelo Carideo is a 10-year veteran social studies educator who teaches literacy through technology integration in New York City. In collaboration with David Liotta and Michael Downes, he has created and runs the Ditmas News Network television show. In addition, he, Downes, and Liotta have developed a series of award-winning student videos that have earned honors at the Celebration for Learning, and the Youth Media Network.

Cathy Collins, a library media specialist for 14 years, works at Sharon High School in Sharon, Massachusetts. She began her career as a reporter who covered business, arts, and education-related issues and has published her writing in various journals including *Library Media Connection* and *NEA Today*. She earned national board certification as a library/media teacher in 2009. ISTE SIG affiliations: SIGLIT, SIGMS (media specialists), and SIGOL (online learning).

Cynthia D. Cummings, EdD, is an assistant professor in the Department of Educational Leadership at Lamar University, Beaumont, Texas. In addition, Cummings serves as an English language arts (ELA) consultant for the Office of Overseas Schools' Project AERO (American Education Reaches Out). Her K–12 experience includes teaching ELA and serving as a district administrator. Cummings is a member of ISTE and the Texas Computer Education Association. Her research interests include global leadership, technology, and e-portfolio use in PK–12. ISTE SIG affiliation: SIGLIT.

Marina Dodigovic has taught English and trained English language leaners (ELL) teachers internationally. Apart from directing ELL and writing programs, she has contributed to the development of American curriculum through writing instruction, and conducted research regarding the uses of technology in second language acquisition. She has a number of publications to her name, including a monograph on the uses of artificial intelligence in second language learning. She is currently teaching at Xi'an Jiaotong-Liverpool University in Jiangsu, China. ISTE SIG affiliation: SIGLIT.

Michael Downes is a former attorney and private investigator, bringing this expertise and a passion for music to his social studies classes. He has created award-winning documentary videos and has collaborated with Angelo Carideo and David Liotta in creating Ditmas News Network in New York City. Downes' innovation has been realized through a Ditmas.tv class book focusing on oral histories of the Holocaust, and through a class book—*Remix of History*—on integrating digital technology and media into Common Core ELA and social studies learning.

Jason J. Griffith has taught eighth grade English at Lamberton Middle School in Carlisle, Pennsylvania since 2003. He is a national board certified teacher and National Writing Project Fellow. An alumnus of the Indiana University of Pennsylvania, Naropa University, and Penn State Harrisburg, Griffith has presented at numerous NCTE conventions as well as state and local workshops. He can be reached by email at BreatheDeepandTeach@gmail.com.

Michele L. Haiken, EdD, teaches at Rye Middle School in Rye, New York, and is an adjunct professor at Manhattanville College in Purchase, New York. A veteran teacher of more than 15 years, she strives to bring digital technology into her classroom with authentic projects that build multiple literacies to bolster student success in the classroom. She is the author of the blog The Teaching Factor (www.theteachingfactor.com) and consults under the name The Teaching Factor (Michele@theteachingfactor.com). ISTE SIG affiliations: SIGLIT and SIGILT (innovative learning technologies).

Troy Hicks, PhD, is an associate professor of English at Central Michigan University (CMU) and focuses his work on the teaching of writing, literacy, and technology, as well as teacher education and professional development. A former middle school teacher, he collaborates with K–12 colleagues. Hicks is director of CMU's Chippewa River Writing Project, a site of the National Writing Project. He is author of *Crafting Digital Writing* (Heinemann, 2013), *The Digital Writing Workshop* (Heinemann, 2009) and a coauthor of *Because Digital Writing Matters* (Jossey-Bass, 2010).

Steven Katz, a technology integration specialist at an international school in Seoul, Korea, has taught all core subjects during his career. Katz has a special interest in instructional movie projects and authored a book to assist teachers in integrating them into the curriculum *Teach with Video* (Katz, 2006). An Apple Distinguished Educator, Katz provides professional development to various schools and presents at conferences internationally and online. Many samples of his and his students' work can be viewed at stevenkatz.com and on his Teach with Video blog (http://teachwithvideo.com/blog). Katz is affiliated with several SIGs: SIGLIT, SIG1to1 (1:1 computing), SIGDS (digital storytelling), SIGETC (educational technology coaches), SIGGS (games and simulations), SIGIS (independent schools), SIGILT (innovative learning technologies), SIGTE (teacher educators), and SIGTC (technology coordinators).

Leah Larson is a library media specialist at Perpich Center For Arts Education Library, Golden Valley, Minnesota, and troop leader for a Latinas Unidas Girl Scout troop. She has been a teacher for nine years, working in special education, ELL, and language arts in Texas and New York, as well as Minnesota. She enjoys her work and collaborating on a variety of projects with her school's excellent teaching staff.

Jennifer Latimer works at the Clinton Elementary School Library in Maplewood, New Jersey. She is completing her master's degree in library and information sciences at Rutgers University and has a BA from Penn State University. Before teaching she was an employee of the Maplewood Memorial Library and spent many years working in the automotive industry. Jennifer can be contacted at jenniferslatimer@gmail.com or visit www.anywherelibrarian.com. ISTE SIG affiliation: SIGLIT.

David Liotta is a social studies educator who also has been a rap performer and is a videographer. Together with Angelo Carideo and Michael Downes, he spearheaded the highly successful Ditmas News Network in New York City and has crafted several winning videos on topics ranging from free speech to the Holocaust.

Diane R. Mason, PhD, is an assistant professor of educational leadership for the online doctoral program at Lamar University, Texas. Her professional experiences consist of teaching K–8 and special education, instructing online graduate students in educational technology leadership and administration, and leading as a middle school assistant principal, elementary principal, and district technology training coordinator. Mason is an ISTE member and past president of the Louisiana ISTE affiliate, LACUE, and past president of Texas Computer Education Association. Her research interests include the Inter/National Coalition for Electronic Portfolio Research; collaboration, technology, and leadership in using Web 2.0 tools; online learning; and reflective professional development. ISTE SIG affiliation: SIGLIT.

B.J. Neary is a high school librarian at Abington Senior High in Abington, Pennsylvania. She is a member of the Pennsylvania State Librarian's Association (PSLA). She curates on Scoop.it! (www.scoop.it/t/young-adult-novels) and she blogs on Goodreads (www.goodreads.com). ISTE SIG affiliations: SIGLIT and SIGMS (media specialists).

Tim Oldakowski is an assistant professor in the English Department at Slippery Rock University in Slippery Rock, Pennsylvania, where he teaches courses in both English education methods and English. His research focuses on multimodal instruction and assessment. He is an active member of the NCTE and his work has been published in the *Journal of Media Literacy Education*. You can follow his blog, Oldakowski's Educational Stuff, which focuses on technology, new literacies, and multimodality in ELA at www.oldakowskiseducationalstuff.blogspot.com.

Mary Paulson is a sixth grade language arts teacher at Richfield Middle School, Minnesota. Prior to teaching sixth grade, she was a literacy coach, a basic skills reading teacher, and a Title I teacher at the elementary level. She is passionate about helping students discover their capabilities in the areas of reading and writing.

Christopher Shamburg is a professor of educational technology at New Jersey City University. He is the author of the books *Student-Powered Podcasting* (ISTE, 2009) and *English Language Arts Units for Grades 9–12* (ISTE, 2008). He is the recipient of several teaching awards, including the 2012 New Jersey Distinguished Faculty Award in Teacher Education. Before working in higher education, he was a high school English teacher for 10 years and earned his doctorate in educational technology from Teachers College, Columbia University. ISTE SIG affiliation: SIGLIT.

Debbie Shoulders teaches middle school English language arts and computer literacy at Northeast Middle School in Clarksville, Tennessee. She has taught for 22 years. Debbie spends her professional development and instructional time pursuing better ways to learn to read and write through technology. She is the author of three books for children. ISTE SIG affiliations: SIGLIT, SIGIVC (interactive videoconferencing), SIGILT (innovative learning technologies), and SIGMS (media specialists).

Salima Smith teaches French at Ditmas Intermediate School 62 in Brooklyn, New York. She came to teaching after a successful career in finance. Smith integrates her love of travel, culture, theater, music, and sports into her teaching. She has taught for 14 years including high school-level French and Spanish in California. A constant in her instruction of students is an emphasis on research-driven and culture-enhanced performance arts components of foreign language. Smith focuses on literacy integration in foreign language.

Contents

Preface..xvii

Introduction..1
    Mark Gura

Authentic Activities..5
Standards for Language Arts and Technology...5
Chapter Descriptions...7

SECTION 1
Reinforcing Reading and Writing with Video and Audio

CHAPTER 1
The Digital-Age Booktalker: Student-Created Digital Book Trailers 15
    B. J. Neary

The Need to Reach All Students..16
Digital Book Trailers Entice Others to Read...17
Using Animoto to Create Student Book Trailers 18
Standards Addressed..22
Conclusion..23
Sample Booktalkers 23
References 24

CHAPTER 2
Creating Online Animations to Pitch Original Short Stories 25
    Cathy Collins

Animation to Sell Their Stories..26
Assessment and Standards Addressed 29
Conclusion: The Impact of Visual Literacy 31

CHAPTER 3
The 20-Shot Short Story 33
    Tim Oldakowski

Background 34
Tech Equipment 35
Implementation..35
Assessment 39

Standards Addressed...40
Conclusion...40

CHAPTER 4

Digital Movie Projects Foster Literacy Growth Across the Curriculum........41
    Steven Katz

Moviemaking: Now an Accessible Classroom Activity.........................42
Organizing and Contextualizing for Successful Classroom Moviemaking 42
Planning, Writing, and Preparing 44
Storyboarding and Scriptwriting 45
Rehearsing, Shooting, and Publishing 48
Standards Addressed..50

CHAPTER 5

Do-It-Yourself Digital 3D Storytelling...53
    Jennifer Latimer

Background 54
Keys to Project Success 55
Procedures..57
Assessment and Standards Addressed 63
Concluding Thoughts 65
References...65

SECTION II
Analyzing and Discussing Literature

CHAPTER 6

Online Literature Circles, Quick Writes, and More................................69
    Debbie Shoulders

Putting the Idea to Work 70
Literacy Applications..71
Literature Circles and More..72
Assessment and Standards Addressed 74
Conclusion..77
Resources 77

CHAPTER 7

Honoring Student Voice Through Blogging...79
  Mary Paulson and Leah Larson

Background 80
Beginning Our Blogging Journey...81
How to Set Up Blogs...83
Beyond the Basics...84
Reflections on the Project..84
Assessment and Standards Addressed 86

SECTION III

Story Writing

CHAPTER 8

Graphic Novel–Style Writing Projects..91
  Mark Gura

Why Graphic Novels? 92
Tools and Techniques..93
Microsoft Word..94
A Wide Variety of Applications 95
A Unique Platform for Improving Writing Skills 96
Standards Addressed...97
Conclusion...100

CHAPTER 9

Interactive Fiction 101
  Gerald W. Aungst

IF = Excitement and Motivation for Reading and Writing 102
Learning with Interactive Fiction...103
Resources Required...105
Implementation...105
From Reader to Writer..106
Student Population...107
Student Work Sample..107
Assessment and Standards Addressed 109
Further Reading..110

CHAPTER 10

Language Learning between the Panels:
Comics, Performance, Shakespeare, and ELL... 111
    Christopher Shamburg

A Tale of Two Comics 112
Technology 113
Shakespeare, Comics, and Performance 114
ELL and Special Needs 116
Assessment and Standards Addressed 117
Conclusion... 119
References 119

SECTION IV
Persuasive and Argumentative Writing

CHAPTER 11

Building Literacy Radiolab-Style:
Podcasting to Foster Speech and Debate Skills..................................... 123
    Michele L. Haiken

Background of Practice 124
Setting Things Up 125
Writing, Recording, and Editing 131
Assessment and Standards Addressed 131
Conclusion: Learning from the NPR Radiolab Model.............................. 134
References 135

CHAPTER 12

Crafting an Argumentative Essay with Evernote..................................... 137
    Troy Hicks

Mrs. Smith's Digital Writing Workshop... 138
The Context for Writing with the Common Core State Standards 139
Beginning the Research Process with Evernote 140
Capturing Sources, Documenting the Process....................................... 141
In the Field, Capturing Other Sources 144
Pulling Her Research Together.. 145
Assessment and Standards Addressed 146
References 148

CHAPTER 13

Enhancing the Argument:
Using Threaded Discussion as a Persuasive Prewriting Tool................... 151
   Jason J. Griffith

Background 152
Teaching and Learning Persuasive Writing through Blogging........................... 153
Managing Online Conversations.. 154
Assessment 155
Standards Addressed... 157
Conclusion.. 158
Resources 159

CHAPTER 14

Building Literacy with Popular Web 2.0 Tools.. 161
   Sheryl R. Abshire, Cynthia D. Cummings,
   Diane R. Mason, and L. Kay Abernathy

Blogging to Support Struggling Writers.. 163
Fostering Collaboration in Literacy Learning with Edmodo............................. 167
Stimulating Interest in and Analysis of Writing with Wordle........................... 171
Promoting Reading Fluency with Audacity 175
Conclusion.. 178
References 178

SECTION V
And Even More Inspiration

CHAPTER 15

Literacy Growth through Digital Television News Production................... 183
   Angelo Carideo, Michael Downes, and David Liotta

A Flexible Model... 184
Not Just Fun Media Projects, but Effective Instructional Practice 185
Equipment Needs 186
Learning the Craft of Video News Production 186
Practice Primer 187
Assessment and Standards Addressed 188
Conclusion: College Readiness and Other Real-World Connections 192
References 192

CHAPTER 16

Providing Feedback in the Writing Process
with Digital Audio and Video 193
William L. Bass

Feedback Is Critical 194
Audio Feedback 194
Video Feedback 197
Standards Addressed 199
Conclusions 200
Resources 201

CHAPTER 17

Using Online Vocabulary Resources
to Improve Pre-College ESL and SAT Literacy Skills 203
Marina Dodigovic

The Importance of Vocabulary in Understanding Meaning 204
Vocabulary Journaling Activity 205
Example: From Story Reading to Story Writing 210
Additional Writing Activities 212
Assessment 212
Standards Addressed 213
Conclusion 214
References 214

CHAPTER 18

Podcasting in Foreign Language Class 217
Salima Smith

Podcasting en Français! 218
Standards Addressed 220
Materials and Resources Needed 221
Conclusion 222
Resources 223

APPENDIX

ISTE Standards 225
ISTE Standards for Students (ISTE Standards•S) 225
ISTE Standards for Teachers (ISTE Standards•T) 228

Index 231

Preface

The chapters in this book were all written by educators: teachers or instructional supervisors or those who moved into professional and curriculum development to support teachers and further develop the field of education. All contributing authors have logged a very significant amount of time in the classroom. All are still teaching or directly supporting teachers as full partners in ongoing efforts to develop and implement technology-supported instructional practices.

The idea for this book came from discussions I had with numerous colleagues, as well as the editors at ISTE books. Clearly, there was interest in a collection of exciting, replicable classroom practices focused on literacy learning that take advantage of the ever more ubiquitous communications technologies that surround students and teachers as they live and learn. These practices would be particularly relevant, we felt, if they were written by teachers or those who support them directly, in a colleague-to-colleague manner.

I had previously co-edited a compendium of articles for ISTE highlighting technology use for literacy instruction that had been published under the title *Making Literacy Magic Happen: The Best of* Learning & Leading with Technology *on Language Arts*. Although popular for years, it was eventually retired from print. Instructional technology is a dynamic, changing field and what was relevant when it was published, eventually became tired and outmoded. This book is an attempt to pick up the thread and is comprised of 18 chapters, each highlighting a technology-based practice or resource with great promise for K–12 literacy instruction.

Outreach to potential contributing authors was accomplished primarily through the newsletter and wiki of the ISTE Literacy Special Interest Group (SIGLIT). Many members of the SIG contributed to the book or reached out to their own network of colleagues, spreading the call for articles. In fact, many of the contributing authors are also members of other ISTE SIGs, groups that range in focus from media specialists (SIGMS), to teacher educators (SIGTE), to innovative learning technologies (SIGILT). These SIG affiliations are listed in the contributor profiles.

All of this attests to the wide body of interests, experience, and expertise represented here. The breadth of experience included is also clear from the geographic locations of the contributors who hail from such diverse places as Louisiana, Minnesota, Pennsylvania, Texas, New York, New Jersey, Tennessee, Missouri, Massachusetts, Florida, China, and South Korea.

The call for submissions requested chapters describing practices of interest to literacy specialist teachers as well as teachers of other subjects across the curriculum who make fostering literacy an important goal. Of interest would be practices adaptable to the instructional needs of many grade and ability levels. These would feature the use of technology resources that are commonly available for the typical classroom and that address instructional goals defined by state and national standards, including ELA, ISTE Standards for Students, content area standards, and the Common Core State Standards. We sought practices that are immediately useful to teachers in the areas of reading, writing, speaking, and listening, particularly those involving authentic projects in which students produce real literacy products (e.g., books, magazines, online content items, podcasts, videos) to present to real audiences. All chapters would explain how technology facilitates learning, increases motivation, and changes the nature of teaching and learning and how that new knowledge is applied.

Resulting submissions included descriptions of practices that apply technology to classic activities but that heighten their relevance, engagement, and efficacy, as well as practices that focus on aspects of literacy that have changed because of the emergence and impact of technology. All have high potential to be successfully adopted and adapted by classroom teachers.

Covered here is a wide range of practices, including book trailers, persuasive writing, story writing, argumentative essays, digital storytelling, graphic novel projects, and more. Student products that result from these activities include numerous varieties of digital videos, slide presentations, blogs, comics, podcasts, and text items. Many types of media resources are used in the activities, including video, audio, and other media sharing resources, word processing, video- and audio-editing software, as well as tools for online publishing. Other types of instructional resources used in the practices include vocabulary search tools, gaming resources, collaboration and social networking resources, interactive fiction software, and note-taking and archiving resources.

This book presents a body of practice that represents a snapshot of important trends in technology-supported literacy instruction. It also represents a trove of good-to-go instructional activities ready for classroom implementation. All indicate the technology resources required—the vast majority of which are either free, low-cost, or already commonly available in schools—as well as information on implementation, how to assess the student work they generate, and how they align to important educational standards. Thus, the book stands ready to inform and guide educators as they redefine literacy instruction as something that is very much a part of our technology-shaped world.

—Mark Gura

Introduction

Mark Gura

C an we provide our students with educational experiences that are truly worthy of their attention? Can we engage them in activities that will prepare them to be successful in the various dimensions of their lives, particularly as lifelong learners? The authors of the chapters in this book think so. The practices they share in these pages are steeped in their direct experience in making these goals a reality in their classrooms.

Between the covers of this book is a large body of approaches, activities, and resources. This material will intrigue and delight many educators who've been looking for ways to apply a growing body of recently developed technology resources to the needs of classrooms that still have one foot in the world of traditional instruction.

On the pages that follow you'll find practices and approaches to implement curriculum and foster standards-based learning of required content and skills. Because these are not lesson plans per se, there is a great deal of flexibility in how they can be adapted to your own practice. These activities were developed for classes that range from elementary through high school and are labeled as elementary (ELEM), middle school (MS), and high school (HS) grades in Table I.1. However, the majority of the activities can be adapted to use at any of these levels, as well as for English language learners (ELL) and special needs students, so long as the activities are implemented with ability-appropriate vocabulary and performance expectations commensurate with age and grade level capabilities and that the teacher makes certain that students are familiar with and adept at required foundation skills and concepts.

Table I.1 Titles, Technologies, and Grade Levels

Chapter (Activity) Title	School Level			Technologies
	ELEM (Ages 5–10)	MS (Ages 11–14)	HS (Ages 15–18)	
1. The Digital-Age Booktalker: Student-Created Digital Book Trailers			✓	Goodreads.com Online animation • Animoto
2. Creating Online Animations to Pitch Original Short Stories		✓	✓	Online animation • Animoto
3. The 20-Shot Short Story		✓	✓	Digital video • digital camera or smartphone Wikispaces.com
4. Digital Movie Projects Foster Literacy Growth across the Curriculum	✓	✓	✓	Digital video • video recording device • movie-editing software
5. Do-It-Yourself Digital 3D Storytelling	✓	✓	✓	PowerPoint animation • PowerPoint • microphone • digital camera • Soungle
6. Online Literature Circles, Quick Writes, and More		✓		Social networking • Edmodo • Ning • CoveritLive • TodaysMeet
7. Honoring Student Voice Through Blogging		✓		Blogging platforms • 21Classes • Weebly

Table I.1 Continued

Chapter (Activity) Title	School Level			Technologies
	ELEM (Ages 5–10)	MS (Ages 11–14)	HS (Ages 15–18)	
8. Graphic Novel–Style Writing Projects		✓	✓	Mixed graphic and text application of word processing software • MS Word or Apache OpenOffice word processor
9. Interactive Fiction		✓	✓	Digital games • interactive fiction (IF) software
10. Language Learning between the Panels: Comics, Performance, Shakespeare, and ELL		✓		Online comic strip creation • Pixton or other online comics creator
11. Building Literacy Radiolab-Style: Podcasting to Foster Speech and Debate Skills		✓		Podcasting • Radiolab podcast archive • Audacity • Sound Jay • Naturesongs.com
12. Crafting an Argumentative Essay with Evernote		✓	✓	Online information gathering and organizing • Evernote
13. Enhancing the Argument: Using Threaded Discussion as a Persuasive Prewriting Tool		✓		Blogging • Edublogs
14. Building Literacy with Popular Web 2.0 Tools	✓	✓	✓	Various technologies • blogging • Edmodo • Wordle • Audacity

Table I.1 Continued

Chapter (Activity) Title	School Level			Technologies
	ELEM (Ages 5–10)	MS (Ages 11–14)	HS (Ages 15–18)	
15. Literacy Growth through Digital Television News Production		✓		Web-based TV production • digital video camera • Magix Movie Edit Pro (or other video-editing software)
16. Providing Feedback in the Writing Process with Digital Audio and Video	✓	✓	✓	Online and computer-based audio recording, posting, and sharing resources • Vocaroo • Audioboo • Camtasia • Jing • Vimeo
17. Using Online Vocabulary Resources to Improve Pre-College ESL and SAT Literacy Skills			✓	Online text analysis tools • Compleat Lexical Tutor
18. Podcasting in Foreign Language Class		✓		Podcasting • cell phone with recording capability • Audacity • GarageBand

Authentic Activities

The contributors offer activities that students will find relevant, interesting, and in which they'll want to participate. In many ways it's the use of technology that makes this happen. And while the technology itself may be of interest to the students, more often it is the *authentic nature of the types of activities that it makes possible* that offers the greatest value. In these pages we'll see how technology makes it easy for students to create their own TV shows, podcasts, print and screen-based publications, comic strips, and a host of other authentic media items—all things that students find appealing and engaging.

Students will relate to these practices, enjoy them, and embrace them. They can be adopted by a broad range of practitioners, as their focus is on general approaches to activities. In the aggregate, these practices represent a broad and powerful vision of how our classrooms are evolving into a new instructional landscape.

Can we redefine and reestablish school-based learning so that it's engaging, enlightening, and inspiring? Can we find ways to foster a love of learning, as well as an understanding of what learning is and why it's important? Can we give our students experiences that will make them confident, independent learners? I say, "Yes!" and I hope after reading this book you'll agree with me.

Standards for Language Arts and Technology

Common Core State Standards for ELA

The Common Core State Standards, an initiative that is about to redefine a good deal of what goes on in the intellectual lives of our students, is more than just another, better, standards document. Beyond improving on the work of its predecessor documents, which defined what students should learn and how well they should learn it, The Common Core standards, from the outset, are intended to change the focus of what to engage students in and how. That said, of immediate interest to teachers and those who support and supervise them, will be the creation of worthwhile instructional activities as vehicles by which the goals of the Common Core standards may be met.

The Common Core standards come out of new perceptions about the types and depth of learning and understanding required by today's students. This is happening in the same world that in so many ways is informed and shaped by continually more ubiquitous information and communications technologies. It follows then, that students would benefit greatly from using technology to learn ways to function in a world that is shaped by it.

The Common Core standards may be seen by many as yet another layer of more work and more difficulty imposed on what teachers and students have to do to be successful. However, I hope that once specific practices about how to accomplish all this are seen and reflected on, especially as they are presented in the many practices in this book, the Common Core standards will be seen instead as a rationale for doing wonderful projects and activities that foster student expression and creativity and that are highly engaging.

Activities in this book address the following Common Core State Standards (CCSS) for English language arts (ELA):

L   Language

W   Writing

SL   Speaking and Listening

RL   Reading: Literature

RI   Reading: Informational Text

RF   Reading: Foundational Skills

Common Core State Standards for ELA are not limited to traditional English language arts:

> The Standards set requirements not only for English language arts (ELA) but also for literacy in history/social studies, science, and technical subjects." (para. 5, www.corestandards.org/ELA-Literacy)

Technology Standards: ISTE Standards•S and AASL

The practices presented here represent the actionable confluence of technology resources and literacy instructional practices. In each, one or more commonly available technology resource is employed to satisfy an instructional need defined by the standard curriculum and Common Core State Standards for ELA. Further, the practices provide opportunities for students to satisfy the ISTE Standards for Students (formerly the NETS for Students). In many ways these practices are emblematic of progressive educational activities and 21st-century learning goals, such as those outlined in the American Association of School Librarians (AASL) Standards for the 21st-Century Learner.

All practices are mainstream in the sense that they are not conceived of as extra, enrichment oriented activities, but as the principal approaches by which students are to learn central parts of the curriculum. While the technology resources involved are essential to the design and value of the practice, none of the activities included make the use of these resources their prime rationale. None represent efforts to find useful applications of attractive technologies as an end unto themselves. Rather, the technology and its application to a teaching and learning need represent a significant advantage or improvement to established, traditional instructional approaches.

Language Arts Standards for Other Languages

The final chapter, Podcasting in Foreign Language Class, addresses communication standards from the New York State Learning Standards for Languages Other than English (LOTE) (www.p12.nysed.gov/ciai/lote/pub/lotelea.pdf). Smith combines 21st-century technology (podcasting) with the ELA literacy skill of interrogatives in her French One classes.

Chapter Descriptions

The 18 chapters in this book are divided into five sections. Tables I.2–I.6 give a brief description of each chapter, literacies, and types of standards addressed: Common Core State Standards for ELA (CCSS), ISTE Standards for Students (ISTE Standards•S), American Association for School Librarians Standards for the 21st-Century Learner (AASL), and New York State Learning Standards for Languages Other than English (LOTE).

Table I.2 Section I: Reinforcing Reading and Writing with Video and Audio

Chapter Activity Description	Standards Addressed			Literacy
	AASL	ISTE•S	CCSS	
1. Supporting young readers in selecting high interest books, as well as making book recommendations to peers through student created online book trailers.	✓	✓		Book-length fiction, nonfiction, verse
2. Using online animation to provide digital storytelling experiences that involve original student art, writing, and sound.		✓	✓	Short story writing, digital storytelling
3. Digital video creation as a way to foster comprehension through summarization and analysis of literature.		✓		Short story analysis, film literacy
4. Applying simple but authentic digital video methods, students create a variety of video projects that impact their literacy learning strongly.			✓ (W, SL, & L)	Story writing
5. Using online animation to provide digital storytelling experiences that involve original student art, writing, and sound.	✓	✓	✓ (SL)	Digital storytelling, including text, sound effects, and visuals

Table I.3 Section II: Analyzing and Discussing Literature

Chapter Activity Description	Standards Addressed		Literacy
	ISTE•S	CCSS	
6. Integrating a variety of social networking resources and approaches to using them in order to positively impact writing and the other dimensions of literacy learning.	✓	✓ (SL)	Literature circles
7. Facilitating response to literature by fostering improved reading comprehension and writing skills through blogging.	✓	✓ (RL)	Discussions of literature

Table I.4 Section III: Story Writing

Chapter Activity Description	Standards Addressed		Literacy
	ISTE•S	CCSS	
8. Students produce original stories or functional writing using common word processing software to create exciting, text-rich graphic novel–style projects.	✓	✓ (W)	Story writing, report writing, illustrating
9. Using Interactive Fiction software to foster improved writing skills.	✓	✓ (W & RL)	Story reading, story writing
10. Focusing on student and teacher created comic strips, students gain deep insight into important literacy skills.	✓	✓ (RL, W, SL, & L)	Reading, writing, performing

Table I.5 Section IV: Persuasive and Argumentative Writing

Chapter Activity Description	Standards Addressed		Literacy
	ISTE•S	CCSS	
11. Building literacy Radiolab-style: podcasting to foster speech and debate skills.	✓	✓	Speech and debate, informative writing, persuasive writing
12. Employing online information organization tools to mentor students in improving writing informational text.	✓	✓ (W)	Crafting an argumentative essay
13. Required writing to persuade is enhanced and made relevant and highly motivating through a number of approaches using free Web 2.0 resources.	✓	✓ (W)	Essay writing
14. A quartet of easy-to-implement, essential literacy practices that take advantage of free, teacher and student friendly resources.	✓	✓ (W, RI, & RF)	Persuasive writing

Table 1.6 Section V: And Even More Inspiration!

Chapter Activity Description	Standards Addressed			Literacy
	ISTE•S	CCSS	LOTE	
15. Writing, performing, and producing online news to impact numerous essential areas of literacy learning.		✓ (RL, W, SL, & L)		Video news production and broadcasting
16. Recording and embedding sound into student writing to offer improved and personalized feedback.	✓ (also ISTE•T)	✓ (RI, W, SL, & L)		Writing feedback
17. Using sophisticated online tools to analyze text for patterns of word use in order to reflect on and improve vocabulary and its use in writing assignments.	✓	✓		Vocabulary, especially ESL/ELL
18. Teaching interrogatives and their use through student created podcasts.			✓	Foreign language

SECTION I

REINFORCING
reading and writing
WITH VIDEO AND AUDIO

CHAPTER 1

The Digital-Age Booktalker: Student-Created Digital Book Trailers
Grades 10–12 / Ages 15–18 / High School
Goodreads.com, Animoto

CHAPTER 2

Creating Online Animations to Pitch Original Short Stories
Grades 9–12 / Ages 14–18 / High School
Animoto

CHAPTER 3

The 20-Shot Short Story
Grades 6–12 / Ages 11–18 / Middle and High School
Digital camera or smartphone, wikispaces.com

CHAPTER 4

Digital Movie Projects Foster Literacy Growth across the Curriculum
Grades 2–12 / Ages 7–18 / Elementary, Middle, and High School
Video-recording device, movie-editing software

CHAPTER 5

Do-It-Yourself Digital 3D Storytelling
Grades 3–12 / Ages 7–18 / Elementary, Middle, and High School
PowerPoint, microphone, digital camera, Soungle

CHAPTER 1

The Digital-Age Booktalker
Student-Created Digital Book Trailers

B. J. Neary

LEVEL
Grades 10–12 / Ages 15–18 / High School

TECHNOLOGIES
Goodreads.com, Animoto

LITERACY
Book-length fiction, nonfiction, verse

STANDARDS
AASL, ISTE Standards•S

Booktalks are a successful way for librarians to create student interest in reading books. "A booktalk is like a movie preview—it piques a student's interest in reading a book" (Young, 2006). Librarians have historically booktalked in limited ways. Students may come to the library, or librarians bring a cart of books to classrooms to conduct print-based booktalks and suggest appropriate reading materials. A librarian's enthusiasm may ignite a reader's interest for just the right book, or create interest in a particular genre.

The Need to Reach All Students

I've always taken seriously my mission of being the school booktalker. In order to be effective as the booktalker, I read young adult literature in all genres. Goodreads (www.goodreads.com) is a social networking site that allows users to share book recommendations, join groups, participate in book discussions, see what friends are reading, keep track of what they've read, and organize books into virtual bookshelves. I belong to many different Goodreads groups such as *YA Reads for Teachers and Any Other Adults, Young Adult Fiction, Best Teen Books* and *The Book Challenge.* These groups help me stay current as new books are published. Within groups there are discussions and threads where members post what they've read and generate discussions.

I've been blogging on Goodreads since 2007. This networking tool helps me identify good young adult books to read. I also follow young adult book blogs like Reading Rants!, YA Books and More, and Teen Reads. Education blogs (like Joyce Valenza's NeverEnding Search Blog, Richard Byrne's Free Technology for Teachers, and Buffy Hamilton's The Unquiet Librarian) help me to find the latest ideas on educational applications of free web resources. It is essential to stay abreast of the many changes in reading and literacy, and these posts are quite informative. When I discover useful posts, I share and discuss them with my senior high teachers, and we often collaborate on lessons as a result.

I am one of two librarians in our senior high school (Grades 10–12). I've been privileged to bring my love of reading and the wonder of books to our students for the past ten years. Our student population includes reluctant learners, ELL, and special education students, as well as ravenous readers of popular contemporary literature.

In our district, there are three wonderful reading teachers who oversee students who have not sufficiently mastered reading. These students come to the library three to four times a year and I booktalk different genres as requested by their reading teacher. Genre examples include realistic fiction (a favorite), multicultural fiction, mystery, historical fiction, nonfiction (including biography), and novels in verse. With the teacher's input, I focus on the books I think will "grab" the students' interest and turn them into willing readers—it only takes one book to do that!

Many of these students have had limited success with reading, so I promote interesting, fast-paced books that deal with compelling teen-life situations. To fill this need, our library offers multiple copies of the Bluford Series, the Orca Series, and Sharon Draper's Hazelwood High Trilogy. These books are smaller volumes than the average book and are designed with a larger font and eye-catching covers. Such details can be very important to students who are reluctant readers. Some students have enjoyed *The Bully* from the Bluford Series so much that they continue to read many of the other fifteen titles in the series! When booktalking to reluctant readers, it is helpful to tell them that other students have enjoyed the series; students will often try reading a novel knowing peers liked it.

To spark the interest of reluctant readers, it is crucial to have a mechanism with which to extend my reach. Digital book trailers have helped tremendously, providing a type of short-form booktalk.

Digital Book Trailers Entice Others to Read

Not only do we find that showing students digital book trailers is a great way to spark interest in reading specific titles, we take this approach an important step further: we assign students to create their own book trailers. They understand that an important dimension to this assignment is that the book trailers they create will be used to inform and motivate other students to read those same books.

In my role as the school booktalker, I've seen the digital book trailer take off as a way for students to create an original and compelling response to their independent reading task. Creating book trailers is a differentiated way students can demonstrate their knowledge about and understanding of books in a way that plays to their strengths and interests. User-friendly, widely available technology allows students to access and use photographs, music, and text to communicate what they've come to understand and want others to know about a book they've read. Let's take a look at how our teachers do digital book trailer projects with our students.

Using Animoto to Create Student Book Trailers

The creation of these videos has been a very successful way to integrate 21st-century skills that embrace technology, creativity, and critical thinking. It has energized students and teachers to effectively communicate a book's story without giving away the ending. There are a number of school-friendly movie-making programs that can be used for this, including iMovie, Movie Maker, and PhotoStory. My favorite digital book trailer resource is Animoto (www.animoto. com). Animoto offers a free version to educators, which provides access for up to 50 students who may create unlimited videos of any length for a six-month period.

Our school has used Animoto extensively for the past four years; it is the school's most popular free web resource. The final product students generate with Animoto is a video slideshow with music. Animoto lives up to its promise:

> Turning your photos and video clips into professional video slideshows in minutes, free and shockingly simple—we make awesome easy.

Preparation

In their classrooms, teachers log on to the school library site and display digital book trailers created by other students, which are linked to the titles of books in the library catalog. We use several outstanding digital book trailers to showcase exemplary work and discuss what went into producing them (pictures, spelling, giving credit, music, and effects). In this way, students can see the quality of work expected in the final product. Students are motivated when they see other students' videos on the automated circulation system. Teachers can use this as an incentive: "If your digital book trailer is good, it too will be featured in the library catalog." We had 77 student-created book trailers in our 2013 catalog and the number continues to grow.

To prepare their students to think like movie producers, the reading teachers have their students use storyboards that will help them think about the beginning, middle, and end of their digital book trailer.

Animoto Basics

There are a few simple steps to using Animoto. Once the students enter their free educational Animoto code, they will be able to choose from many visual backgrounds. It is important for students to think about the types of pictures needed to tell the story without giving away the ending. Students look for images that will illustrate characters, setting, conflict, climax, and a cliffhanger or question. For our book trailers, we have students provide the cover of the book at the beginning and again at the end of the trailer.

Most digital book trailers are one minute long, but they may be longer depending on how many pictures the teacher requires (usually 10–15). A good rule to follow while looking for images is to be sure the images are at least 640 × 480 dpi in resolution, which will give a professional, clear (not pixelated) image in the video when the book trailer is enlarged to screen size for classroom or individual computer viewing.

It is important to use images that are licensed in Creative Commons or available for free use. Some good image sites to search are Flickr.com, FreeFoto.com, and Morguefile.com. Once students have saved images to their folders, it is important to provide credit for each image. Students should copy the image's source URL and paste it into a PowerPoint slide to begin a "Works Cited" or "Mediagraphy" slide that will hold all the identifying information. This will be the final slide included in the book trailer.

Once all the pictures have been imported into Animoto, students can move them around and use Animoto's Rotate, Spotlight, and Duplicate functions to enhance the images. Two lines of text can be added to describe each image. Students may find this type of abbreviated description limiting, but teachers can emphasize how the photo is telling the story and the text, while being critical, needs to be succinct.

Adding Music

The final part of creating the Animoto video requires choosing music to match the mood of the book. I always recommend that our students use Animoto's very large and varied music archive (more than 600 music tracks across dozens of genres) since their music is Creative Commons licensed or royalty free. If students upload their own MP3 music, attribution is required, the same as it is for the images.

Fair use copyright law permits some use of copyrighted material in educational, not-for-profit, classroom settings. Students' use of copyrighted songs and images in the Animoto assignments is questionable and may or may not fall under fair use if the book trailer is posted online. This is a good opportunity to discuss copyright infringement with your students. Below is an excerpt from the Animoto's terms of service web page:

> You agree that you will not upload, share, or otherwise distribute any Submissions—including text, graphics, images, sounds, data, music, or other information—that … are to be used for a commercial purpose of any kind. (www.animoto.com/legal/terms)

Rendering the Final Video

Finalization of the Animoto video is known as rendering. There are three different resolutions to choose from for faster- or slower-paced videos. Each Animoto video is totally customized; no two videos are the same. And if a student doesn't like the speed or finds they have misspelled a word or just wants a different video, there is an Edit feature that will generate a new video. Students, like movie producers, become aware that timing is crucial and when done right, will result in creating an exciting digital book trailer that could have other students vying to read the book. Students will have the link of the final version emailed to them. Each video is then shown in class, where all discuss and review it, guided by a rubric (Table 1.1).

Table 1.1 Rubric for Assessing Final Videos

Category	Full credit	Partial credit	Half credit	Zero credit
Images 30 points	Images depict story elements accurately; use of at least 10 images, as well as cover of the book.	Use of 10 images, but some of the images do not fit in with the story.	Very few of the images fit in with the story, or there are fewer than 10 images used.	Images do not fit in with the story, or there are fewer than 7 images used.
Content of the Book (captions) 35 points	Captions go along with images and accurately tell the story in the student's own words.	Almost all content is in the student's own words and is accurate. There is some correlation between images and captions, but there are gaps in the story.	At least half of the content is in the student's own words and is accurate. Captions are incomplete and do not tell most of the story.	Less than half of the content is in the student's own words and/or is accurate. Captions are inadequate and reveal very little knowledge of the story.
Quality 10 points	No spelling or grammatical mistakes on a storyboard with lots of text. Captions are easily read; images are clear and video lasts at least 1 minute.	1–3 spelling or grammatical mistakes on a storyboard with little text. One or more images are blurry and/or captions cannot be read clearly.	3–5 spelling or grammatical errors on the storyboard. Several slides are blurry with unclear captions. Lasts less than 1 minute.	More than 5 spelling and/or grammatical errors on the storyboard. Most slides are blurry with unclear captions.
Music 10 points	Clean version of a song that goes along with the story.	Clean version of a song, but it does not fit in with the story.	Poor version of a song.	No music is included or an inappropriate song is used.
Credit Slide 15 points	A credit slide is included as the last slide, giving credit to ALL the websites where pictures and music were found.	A credit slide is included as the last slide; giving credit to some of the websites where pictures and music were found.	A credit slide is included as the last slide, but it only gives credit to 1–5 websites.	A credit slide is not included.

Standards Addressed

American Association of School Librarians (AASL) Standards for the 21st Century Learner:

2. Learners use skills, resources, and tools to: Draw conclusions, make informed decisions, apply knowledge to new situations, and create new knowledge.

    2.1 *Skills*

    2.1.4 Use technology and other information tools to analyze and organize information.

    2.1.6 Use the writing process, media and visual literacy, and technology skills to create products that express new understandings.

ISTE Standards for Students (ISTE Standards•S)

1. **Creativity and Innovation**

    Students demonstrate creative thinking, construct knowledge, and develop innovative products and processes using technology. Students:

    a. apply existing knowledge to generate new ideas, products, or processes

    b. create original works as a means of personal or group expression

2. **Communication and Collaboration**

    Students use digital media and environments to communicate and work collaboratively, including at a distance, to support individual learning and contribute to the learning of others. Students:

    a. interact, collaborate, and publish with peers, experts, or others employing a variety of digital environments and media

3. **Research and Information Fluency**

    Students apply digital tools to gather, evaluate, and use information. Students:

    a. plan strategies to guide inquiry

    b. locate, organize, analyze, evaluate, synthesize, and ethically use information from a variety of sources and media

c. evaluate and select information sources and digital tools based on the appropriateness to specific tasks

Conclusion

The need for students to demonstrate comprehension of books they've read is a constant, but for today's reluctant readers, reading is often more of a chore than ever: It's something they must do for school but see little use for beyond academia. Through booktalks, librarians spark interest in reading by discussing topics and genres, a practice that can support students in making the transition to reading for pleasure or to learn for their own interests. The student-created digital book trailer is an even more powerful approach to sparking students' interest in reading.

In this age of e-readers versus traditional, hard-copy books, my mission as a 21st-century booktalker remains very important: to continually put great books into all my students' hands. It makes my librarian heart very happy when, as a result of a booktalk, a student reads a book and is enticed to pick up another and another and another. This is even more the case when one of the student-created book trailers in our school library catalog arouses interest and motivates a student to check out and read a book!

Sample Booktalkers

Darkness Before Dawn: animoto.com/play/UIPS3yfgfZprI6W1CQCCBA

The Gun: http://animoto.com/play/Rpqn5rRSl8oi7raRv89n0w

Juice: http://animoto.com/play/8ZNKYWiVFyQVIjs0nQB43g

Lockdown: animoto.com/play/IVVWlOXfuvfaRtxSCIT0Qw

Rooftop: animoto.com/play/fka0w8vKaGVAMnfHNtdU0Q

Rucker Park Setup: animoto.com/play/g53AMxJEzWmJGlDN5WcdBQ

Sticks and Stones: animoto.com/play/aK0gOouh1Z7sIjf1FfEItw

Swim the Fly: animoto.com/play/TASRirfM1YMdsncwu0brmg

Things Change: animoto.com/play/yEoXBWSGNA358aP7RI8UCQ

References

American Association of School Librarians. (2007). *Standards for the 21st-century learner.* Chicago, IL: Author. Retrieved from www.ala.org/aasl/standards-guidelines/learning-standards

Brehm-Heeger, P. (2008). *Serving urban teens.* Westport, CT: Libraries Unlimited.

Bull, G., & Bell, L. (Eds.). (2010). *Teaching with digital video: Watch, analyze, create.* Eugene, OR: International Society for Technology in Education (ISTE).

Cart, M. (2010). *Young adult literature: From romance to realism.* Chicago, IL: ALA.

Eaton, G. (2002, October) *How to do a book talk.* Paper presented at the Massachusetts School Library Media Association annual conference, Sturbridge, MA. Retrieved from www.uri.edu/artsci/lsc/Faculty/geaton/MSLMAtalk

Fink, M. P. (2012). Come into the house of poetry. *VOYA, 35*(1), 19–20.

Gorman, M., & Suellentrop, T. (2009). *Connecting young adults and libraries.* New York, NY: Neal-Schuman.

International Society for Technology in Education (ISTE). (2007). *National educational technology standards for students (NETS·S)* (2nd ed.). Eugene, OR: Author. Retrieved from www.iste.org/standards/nets-for-students

Ohler, J. (2008). *Digital storytelling in the classroom.* Thousand Oaks, CA: Corwin.

Young, T. E., Jr. (2006). Booktalking: Get your reluctant readers to listen up! *RHInc.: Annual magazine for educators, 1*(1), 28. Revised article originally published in American Association of School Librarians' (AASL) *Knowledge Quest, 32*(1), 2003. Retrieved from www.randomhouse.com/highschool/RHI_magazine/pdf/young.pdf

CHAPTER 2

Creating Online Animations to Pitch Original Short Stories

Cathy Collins

LEVEL

Grades 9–12 / Ages 14–18 / Middle and High School

TECHNOLOGY

Animoto

LITERACY

Short story writing, digital storytelling

STANDARDS

ISTE Standards•S, CCSS for ELA (Key design)

A s a high school library media specialist, I have always been excited about the use of educational technology tools to stimulate students who otherwise might not be overly motivated to read and to write. Although the majority of the students in our school community (Sharon High School in Sharon, Massachusetts) are academically driven, SHS shares at least one concern with most other high schools: Finding ways to engage students in lengthy reading and writing projects can be challenging.

After attending a summer institute on integrating Web 2.0 sources into classroom learning, I became intrigued by the potential of digital tools to transform student perceptions and motivation around reading and writing assignments. As a first step in my commitment to sharing these new tools, I presented a workshop on digital storytelling tools to the SHS English Department. Based on feedback from the workshop, I realized that many of our English teachers were open to the idea of utilizing the Web 2.0 tools I had shared. I found a willing collaborative partner in Lori Ayotte, who teaches a creative writing course at SHS. After an initial planning session, we decided to have students create digital story pitches using Animoto to "pitch" to potential readers the short stories they had just written. We scheduled four sessions in the library for the unit.

Animation to Sell Their Stories

Animoto is a web application that creates professional looking videos with ease. Users simply choose songs, images, or video clips that they'd like to include, and Animoto helps them automatically generate a unique video. No two videos are ever the same. I chose Animoto for the project because it allows students to focus on the creative aspects of matching text to sound and images, without having to learn the technical aspects of video production.

To sign up for an Animoto educator account:

- Go to Animoto's Education site: www.animoto.com/pro/education.

- Click **Sign up now** to obtain an educator's account.

- Provide your name, school email address, grade(s) and subject(s) taught, and school website address.

- Record your classroom promotional code for distribution to students; this code will be emailed to you as well. This code is good for six months and will allow up to 50 students to make full-length videos.

- After the teacher has registered, students can sign up using the promotional code.

To begin our unit, students were given the task of writing a short story. The original story guidelines included these requirements:

- The story should be 3–5 pages long.

- The action should happen over a long weekend.

- The story opens with a line of exposition as the protagonist watches the antagonist arrive.

- The antagonist has something that the protagonist wants or thinks he or she deserves.

- Over the course of the weekend, the protagonist is presented with the opportunity of taking this object of desire … or not.

- Important: This "thing" should have metaphorical value or "suggestiveness." It should be the controlling metaphor and the title of the story.

- Equally as important: Nothing is explained; we are told nothing or almost nothing. Everything (meaning, feeling, thought) unfolds through action, detail, and description.

- Our mantra: "Show, don't tell."

Lori then taught students the basics of *selling* the short stories they had written using animation. She shared the importance of considering audience and purpose before selecting text, images and sound. She also stressed the need to match content and style to an audience, along with the need to hook the audience by carefully considering characters, conflicts, and plot points that should be highlighted.

Students spent two days with me in the library. I taught them the basics of using Animoto and shared examples of videos that were created to entice readers, including those produced by others students as well as professionals. Using the computers available in the library, students began the task of selecting images, adding text and music for emotional impact, and editing their videos as necessary. Lori and I worked individually with students, who had differing levels of expertise in using the technology. Due to the simplicity of Animoto and the visual and auditory elements, we found that students were completely and instantly engaged in creating their videos. I offered technical assistance as necessary for those students who had less experience with video production technology. Students enjoyed experimenting with different transition styles, songs, images, and placement of text.

The act of retelling their own short stories through text, images, and sound added to the students' understanding of the story-making process, as evidenced through journal entries they wrote regularly during the project. Students who were especially knowledgeable about downloading music or selecting images but who might not normally have stepped up to the plate emerged as leaders and were eager to share their knowledge with other students.

Students shared their final video projects in class, so that they could informally give feedback and recognize each other's efforts. Exemplary videos were then displayed internally in an online video gallery featured on the school's Virtual Library website.

Students had the opportunity to share their work with each other, and I shared it informally at meetings with staff and parents. This generated interest among other teachers and further collaborative Web 2.0 projects emerged. One of these involved the use of digital story pitches as an alternative form of assessment for use with special education students. Another project involved students sharing the life stories of artists through use of Glogster EDU (www.glogster.com) and Prezi (www.prezi.com). I highlight examples of all digital storytelling projects on Sharon High School's Virtual Library website (http://shsvirtuallibrary.weebly.com) in the "Teacher Research Projects/Pathfinder" section and "EdLine Library Media Portal" section. References on how to use Web 2.0 tools are listed in the "Just for Teachers" and "Tech Tools and How-to's" sections.

Since this was the first short story assignment for the course, students were naturally enthusiastic about promoting their final products. The use of Animoto provided a further multimedia aspect to their projects, allowing students to solidify their visual literacy and digital literacy skills. Beyond that, Animoto reinforced their understanding of metaphor through their direct incorporation of images to convey meaning in their stories.

Assessment and Standards Addressed

Assessment

Students were assessed on the following:

- Choice of visual images (5 points)

- Choice of music/audio (5 points)

- Word choice (5 points)

- Concision (producing a video not to exceed 2 minutes, 30 seconds) (5 points)

- Incorporation of visual images, sound, and text in an effective manner (5 points)

In addition, students were required to write a reflective journal entry in which they described what they learned from the short story pitch video project and the learning process.

Standards

ISTE Standards for Students (ISTE Standards•S)

All ISTE Standards for Students (www.iste.org/standards/nets-for-students) are addressed in this project:

1. **Creativity and Innovation**

   Students demonstrate creative thinking, construct knowledge, and develop innovative products and processes using technology.

2. **Communication and Collaboration**

   Students use digital media and environments to communicate and work collaboratively, including at a distance, to support individual learning and contribute to the learning of others.

3. **Research and Information Fluency**

   Students apply digital tools to gather, evaluate, and use information.

4. **Critical Thinking, Problem Solving, and Decision Making**

   Students use critical-thinking skills to plan and conduct research, manage projects, solve problems, and make informed decisions using appropriate digital tools and resources.

5. **Digital Citizenship**

   Students understand human, cultural, and societal issues related to technology and practice legal and ethical behavior.

6. **Technology Operations and Concepts**

   Students demonstrate a sound understanding of technology concepts, systems, and operations.

Common Core State Standards for ELA

Regarding the blending of research and media skills into the Common Core State Standards for English Language Arts (ELA) standards as a whole, the CCSS states:

> To be ready for college, workforce training, and life in a techno-logical society, students need the ability to gather, comprehend, evaluate, synthesize, and report on information and ideas, to conduct original research in order to answer questions or solve problems, and to analyze and create a high volume and extensive range of print and non-print texts in media forms old and new. The need to conduct research and to produce and consume media is embedded into every aspect of today's curriculum. In like fashion, research and media skills and understandings are embedded throughout the Standards rather than treated in a separate section. (www.corestandards.org/ELA-Literacy/introduction/key-design-consideration, para. 5)

Conclusion: The Impact of Visual Literacy

American filmmaker George Lucas argues passionately in "Life on the Screen: Visual Literacy in Education" that we must teach communication skills comprehensively, in all forms. He states,

> Today we work with the written or spoken word as the primary form of communication. But we also need to understand the importance of graphics, music, and cinema, which are just as powerful and in some ways more deeply intertwined with young people's culture. We live and work in a visually sophisticated world, so we must be sophisticated in using all the forms of communication, not just the written word. (www.edutopia.org/lucas-visual-literacy, para. 6)

Instructing our students to write short stories and then retell them through sound and images gave them a chance to actualize the "show, don't tell" writer's mantra in an alternative format, thereby reinforcing the concept in their minds. In addition, it allowed them to assess whether they had, in fact, successfully mastered the concept in the written version of their stories.

Lucas also says, "We must accept the fact that learning how to communicate with graphics, with music, with cinema, is just as important as communicating with words" (www.edutopia.org/lucas-visual-literacy, para. 20). The simplicity of using Web 2.0 tools such as Animoto facilitates visual literacy instruction with minimal cost involved. Aside from the purchase of a $30 Animoto Educator classroom account and access to a library media center, computer lab, or laptop/iPad cart, little outside investment is necessary.

By incorporating digital technology into writing instruction, we are expanding student understanding of visual storytelling concepts, and moving art and music out of separate classroom containers and back into English class, where they also belong.

CHAPTER 3

The 20-Shot Short Story

Tim Oldakowski

LEVEL

Grades 6–12 / Ages 11–18 / Middle and High School

TECHNOLOGIES

Digital camera or smartphone, wikispaces.com

LITERACY

Short story analysis, film literacy

STANDARDS

ISTE Standards•S

"Lights! Camera! English class!"

I use these words to pique the interest of students before we read short stories. A typical assessment activity following a unit on a short story might ask students to write a paper in which they summarize what happened in it. While writing is very important, such an assignment only asks students to perform one cognitive skill—summarization. What about analysis? What about asking our students to become critical thinkers? What about asking them to support their arguments? I've found a way to allow students to truly demonstrate their thinking about a short story by asking them to construct a short video adaptation of the story, an activity I call *The 20-Shot Short Story.*

Background

With the presence of signs, symbols, sounds, and images in society today, it's impossible to communicate without understanding how to view, navigate, observe, and listen as well as read and write. Why then, are so many assessments designed to only incorporate writing? While language is a necessary mode, it is not the only mode we see in the world, therefore it should not be the only mode we utilize in schools. This is why I have developed *The 20-Shot Short Story.*

Having taught this activity at both the high school and university levels, I find that students are engaged, work collaboratively, review the text, and produce videos that not only summarize the story, but include a level of analysis that might not come across in a paper. While I currently teach this activity to preservice English language arts (ELA) teachers in a university setting, I feel that this activity could be done in any classroom where students read literature. I suggest grade levels 6–12 because students will have to shoot videos in small groups outside of the classroom for a period or two. Students in earlier grades quite likely are not up to the level of responsibility or independent self-support required to succeed.

Producing *The 20-Shot Short Story* encourages students to reread and review the text so that they have a clear understanding of the material, pick up on small details in the text, and have an understanding of how multiple literary elements are utilized in the short story. By creating a video, students must also work with multiple modalities. Just as writing has its own set of rules, so do the other modes. For example, cinematography requires knowledge of space. Each type of shot and angle used has its own meaning, as do other modalities, such as color and gesture.

Students must understand that the colors they use and the gestures they create as they play characters also reveal how they think about the text. In other words, when students have more modalities from which to work, they have more ways of showing their understanding about the text.

Tech Equipment

Any device that captures video can be used for this project. Again, the emphasis is not necessarily on the quality of the video, rather it is on the modes students use to create that video. A flip-cam works best because it can simply be attached to the computer's USB port and the video can be transferred to the desktop as a QuickTime file.

A high-speed internet connection is also necessary so that students can upload to the internet. There is the option to upload the video to YouTube, either privately or publicly. Because students are minors, one might require parental permission to upload content, even if it is a private channel.

Another option is to have students upload the video to a password protected wiki page, such as Wikispaces Classroom (www.wikispaces.com). That way, access can be limited and all the videos are in one place, which makes screening and assessing them easy to conduct.

Implementation

On the first day of the lesson, I speak with students about the language of film, a language they'll need to learn a bit about in order to respond to the short story they read with an effective video response. I ask them to list specific camera shots and angles (such as close-ups or low angles) that they have seen in film and what they thought these shots or angles represented. I also ask them to consider the way that other elements in film, such as gestures, facial expressions, colors, and props might influence the film. We engage in a discussion about how film has a language all of its own and that these multiple elements of film are purposeful and have a meaning.

Camera Shots and Angles

I then provide the students with some notes on the various types of camera shots and angles and their meanings (Tables 3.1 and 3.2).

Table 3.1 Types of Camera Shots and Their Intended Meanings

Extreme long shot (ELS)	A wide shot that captures the locale and establishes where the action is taking place
Long shot (LS)	The full body of a character; the distance between an audience member and a performer
Medium shot (MS)	A character shot from the waist to the head; establishes a closer relationship to the character
Close up (CU)	A character shot from the shoulders to the head; allows for recognition of facial expressions
Extreme close up (ECU)	The closest the camera can get to an object; places emphasis on the object
Over the Shoulder (OS)	Two individuals are talking and the person in the background is in focus, the person in the foreground has the back of his/her head to the camera; suggests that the character is talking to another character and not the audience

Table 3.2 Types of Camera Angles and Their Intended Meanings

Bird's eye view	Shot from completely overhead; suggests that the subjects on screen are vulnerable or insignificant or that the observer is powerful
High	Shot from above; suggests that the subject on the screen is powerless
Low	Shot from below; suggests that the subject on the screen is powerful or significant
Eye level	Shot of the character at his/her eye level; suggests normalcy; is a clear view of character
Oblique	Camera is tilted on axis; suggests tension, anxiety, or excitement

Storyboarding

After providing information about camera shots and angles, I introduce the students to the concept of storyboarding, which is the sketching out of each shot in a film. I explain that while shooting, time is limited, and most directors have a storyboard that contains sketches of each shot, in consecutive order, so that the director will have an idea where to place the camera and how to shoot the shot. After all, time on the set is valuable!

At the end of the class period, I provide each student with a short story and a blank storyboard with exactly 20 empty shots. I tell the students that they are to assume the role of the director and using the assigned short story, sketch out, in exactly 20 shots, a filmic version of their story. By limiting the shots to 20, everyone has the same framework from which to work. While films should be between two and five minutes, giving them the same limit on shots provides everyone with an equal opportunity to create a filmic version of the story. I typically assign about four or five students to a story, but I do not let them know who has the same story, because I want them to create individual storyboards so that I can see how each student thinks about the text.

On the second day of the lesson, I ask the students to organize by groups according to their assigned stories. I give them the entire class period to compare storyboards and challenge them as a group to come up with a final storyboard that they will shoot the next day. I also tell them that, as we will use in-camera editing, they will have to film the various scenes in the order they appear in the story. Unlike professional filmmakers who shoot out of sequence and assemble the shots later, in-camera editing is a process in which the camera operator simply records a shot and pauses as soon as the shot is completed. Then the director sets up the second shot and records, pausing at the end. Our purpose for in-camera editing is to focus on the analysis of the story.

In an effort to save time, editing is not taught but certainly could be, should a teacher have access to digital-editing tools. A student may also want to edit the film. For the purposes of analysis, though, the emphasis is placed on the language of film, gesture, color and material. This means that students will have multiple modes from which to demonstrate their understanding of the text: language, space, gesture, color and materiality.

Filming

On the third and fourth days of the lesson, I provide students with a digital video camera. Any device that captures digital video will suffice, though I prefer to use a flip-cam because the transition between each shot is smooth. I provide students with an overview of in-camera editing as described above and make sure that each group has a completed storyboard. I also remind students that emphasis must be placed on story analysis, not acting or editing, since the purpose of the video is for them to show their understanding of the short story. Thus, this does not have to be a slick or professional video, but it should present understanding of the story via multiple modes.

Once the students have completed their films, I ask for one volunteer from each group to download it from the camera to a computer, and then upload the video to our class wiki. I have found Wikispaces Classroom (www.wikispaces.com) to be an excellent free site for creating wikis. On the class's home page I have a link titled *The 20 Shot Short Story* where each group's film can be uploaded.

Written Rationale

Once the videos have been shot and uploaded I ask each student to type a one- to two-page rationale in which they discuss their experience with shooting *The 20-Shot Short Story*. I ask them to describe how using additional modalities allowed them to express their thinking. I ask them to consider how image, sound, shot composition, color, and materials helped them to transfer the story from print to video. I also ask them to describe how they came to decide what to leave out and what to include from the story. Then I ask students to describe their overall experience with the making of the video. I leave this open-ended so that students can share their likes, dislikes, challenges, successes, and so on.

Screening

Finally, on the fifth day of the lesson, the students screen the videos. After each group shows their video, I ask them to come to the front of the class, and share some of what they have written in their rationales. This is very informal because it's a way for the whole class to understand how multiple modes affected the transformation of knowledge from print to screen.

Assessment

Students are assessed on three components: the storyboard, the video, and a written rationale (Table 3.3). The purpose of grading the storyboard is so that there is evidence that the students planned out the shots, giving careful consideration to how they were translating the print story to video. The video itself is graded based upon both literary elements and cinematic elements. Finally, the rationale is worth about 20 percent of the final grade.

As students work in groups, I constantly monitor and interact with them to be sure that they are staying on task, but more important, to see if they have any questions. This is when I remind them that we are not looking for a slick or flawless video, but that they are using these additional modes to articulate their understanding of a short story. In other words, the process of filmmaking is more important than the product.

Table 3.3 The Assessment Rubric

Component	Point Value
Storyboard	
Storyboard contained a sketch for each of the 20 shots and shots were labeled with the type of shot and/or angle.	25 points
Video	
The video summarized the plot of the novel.	10 points
Major characters were represented.	10 points
The conflict and resolution were apparent and portrayed.	10 points
A variety of camera shots, angles and movements were used and were essential to the story.	25 points
Rationale	
A 1- to 2-page typed rationale includes justifications for types of shots and angles used and explains why elements were included and/or left out of the video.	20 points

Standards Addressed

ISTE Standards for Students (ISTE Standards•S)

The 20-Shot Short Story addresses the following ISTE Standards•S:

1. **Creativity and Innovation**

   Students demonstrate creative thinking, construct knowledge, and develop innovative products and processes using technology.

2. **Communication and Collaboration**

   Students use digital media and environments to communicate and work collaboratively, including at a distance, to support individual learning and contribute to the learning of others.

4. **Critical Thinking, Problem Solving, and Decision Making**

   Students use critical-thinking skills to plan and conduct research, manage projects, solve problems, and make informed decisions using appropriate digital tools and resources.

6. **Technology Operations and Concepts**

   Students demonstrate a sound understanding of technology concepts, systems, and operations.

Conclusion

The outcomes of *The 20-Shot Story* are many and varied. Not only are the students paying attention to key elements of literature, but they are extending their learning by analyzing how these elements affect the story as well as discussing why they are (or are not) pertinent to the story. They are moving beyond simply noticing elements and are discussing how a story would function differently with or without them. Students also work collaboratively, as this is a prime dimension of sociocultural and constructivist learning. Students also work with 21st-century literacies and technology in a meaningful way that allows them to create—rather than regurgitate—knowledge. *The 20-Shot Short Story* also demonstrates the importance of using multiple modes as a form of assessment because it is through these additional modes that the students' thinking is mediated.

CHAPTER 4

Digital Movie Projects Foster Literacy Growth Across the Curriculum

Steven Katz

LEVEL

Grades 2–12 / Ages 7–18 / Elementary, Middle, and High School

TECHNOLOGIES

Video-recording device, movie-editing software

LITERACY

Story writing

STANDARDS

CCSS for ELA (Writing, *W*; Speaking and Listening, *SL*; and Language, *L*)

n the past fifteen years, I've facilitated movie creation in all core subject areas, Grades 2–12, and also with students in my master's courses. Student motivation and engagement while creating movies is extremely high, and public presentation of the movies keeps students focused on doing their very best work.

Students engaged in the process of moving a story from a rough idea to a finished video project develop speaking, listening, reading, and writing skills. In particular, the process of planning, storyboarding, and scripting a movie mirrors and reinforces traditional writing skills.

Moviemaking: Now an Accessible Classroom Activity

Gaining access to the hardware and software needed to create movies has become much easier in the past five years. Most computers come with some movie-editing software installed. Many handheld devices (tablets, smartphones) also have editing software, and most mobile phones have the capability of shooting video. There are also several movie creation websites that include everything from creating an animation to uploading and editing footage shot on a camera, phone, or computer. My students have used many kinds of hardware, software, and online tools to successfully complete their movies.

Organizing and Contextualizing for Successful Classroom Moviemaking

Curricular goals should be the prime focus for movie projects. While you can use movies effectively as a culminating activity for students to demonstrate their understanding of a particular topic, this chapter focuses on movies as a vehicle for students' original stories.

I've never been overly concerned with the quality of student video, focusing instead on the quality of the content produced. I simply don't believe that a movie needs to look polished in order to foster and demonstrate learning. Still, students are expected to hold the camera steady, use proper lighting, and provide clear sound. However, if your goals for the project include improvement of technology skills, then by all means get students to go as "Hollywood" as they can.

Easy to Challenging Movie Projects

Depending on the skills involved, movie projects that foster literacy can be easy *or* challenging for students to do. The simplest approach involves doing "one-shot" movies, filmed straight through with no editing. The most challenging involves students creating all original material, multiple shooting sessions, and editing. I recommend this approach for students fifth grade and older. Eighth grade students tend to find this an easier task than the fifth, sixth, and seventh graders. It's the most time-consuming type of movie to create, but it also provides the most learning opportunities.

I used to believe that before assigning a technology project to students, teachers should master the software the students will be using. After working with my students and other teachers on many projects, I've seen very successful outcomes when the teacher has only a basic knowledge of the tools the students use. As long as the teacher can provide introductory material and answer general questions, the students are very likely to succeed with the technological aspects of the project. In many cases, the collective knowledge of the class will quickly surpass the teacher's expertise.

Teachers assigning a technology-based project should first create the same project they will ask their students to do. This gives the teacher clear insight as to what goes into the project, the time it takes, the tools needed, and challenges their students may encounter.

A Rubric, Guidelines, and Time Limits

In preparing a movie project assessment rubric, it's important to create clear guidelines. Teachers should focus on curricular goals, but include some technical aspects to ensure the movie is watchable. When done poorly, sound and camera movement are the two aspects that can make the movie unwatchable. Other technical aspects such as lighting, titles, and transitions are not as critical, but you may want to include them in your rubric.

The following resource is designed to help you build rubrics for goals, guidelines, and assessments associated with your classroom moviemaking projects.

Movie rubric creator: www.teachwithvideo.com/movie-rubrics.html

Setting a time limit for the movie is essential as part of the assessment rubric. With younger students, I'd suggest movies that are no more than 1 minute. In middle school, 1–2 minutes is ideal. In high school, depending on the topic and experience of the students, I've seen excellent movies as long as 12 minutes. Time constraints often bring about higher-level thinking. Having to tell a story with many details in a short period of time forces the students to analyze what is essential to the story and create a concise, meaningful summary. Often students will ask me to extend the time limit, but I've found that extensions are almost always a mistake When the movie time is limited, students are compelled to discuss the topic, analyze it, and debate about what should end up in the final cut of the movie—in other words, they must focus on what's really important. After explaining the rubric, I show example movies to the class and we evaluate them based on the rubric. This helps the students have a clear idea about what's expected.

Group versus Individual Productions

Another decision that has to be made by the teacher is to assign the movie as an individual or group project. When the final product is thirty seconds or less, I generally assign this as an individual project. Longer movies seem to be more successful when done in groups. Regardless of whether I assign this as a group or an individual project, I always have students do most of the planning and writing individually. Then I assign them to groups and have them decide on which script they'll produce.

Planning, Writing, and Preparing

When the students begin topic selection, the teacher's guidance and approval of the project is essential. I don't allow students to progress in the project unless they have received my approval. Teachers should assess the work, provide specific feed-back for every step in the process, and have the students make adjustments. Any work that is approved by the due date receives full credit and the student moves on to the next step.

An unfocused topic leads to a poor storyboard and an even worse script. Require students to create a one-sentence topic that has a message. The topic selection will be the basis of all other work that is done on the movie. Examples of good, focused topics might be something like *The Fox and the Stork* (a version of the Aesop's fable) or a story about the actual events of the first Thanksgiving. Do not allow students to choose an ambiguous topic.

Once the topic is set, I have students work on a brief plan for the movie. This helps students to start thinking about all the details of the project. The plan should include the movie topic, a paragraph summary of the plot, the specific filming location, all props and costumes that will be needed, and a list of all the actors and the roles each will play.

I also have students complete a short activity about the different types of camera shots they may use in their movies. There are many websites that explain the different shots; one example is Media College (www.mediacollege.com). Students research the various camera angles and shots, then draw examples of different types of shots. I challenge them to use numerous types of shots from various angles in order to make a more interesting movie.

Storyboarding and Scriptwriting

Storyboarding

Making a storyboard is the next step. I created a storyboard tool, similar to Form 4.1, for my students to use. This tool is available as a PDF on my Teach with Video website:

> **Teach with Video website:** www.teachwithvideo.com

> **Storyboard tool:** http://teachwithvideo.com/download_archives/storyboard1.pdf

The tool asks for shot and location, and provides space for students to sketch what each shot will look like. I allow them to use photos if appropriate. They must define the type of shot and the specific location for the filming. Requiring a specific location, for example, "in front of the lockers," demonstrates a clear, thought-out plan. Students must also include audio details in the storyboard. I ask them to describe everything that will be heard, including script, background noise, music, and sound effects. This is the first time students write lines for the movie.

Storyboard

Name: _____   Title: _____

Audio:	Shot:
	Location:

Audio:	Shot:
	Location:

Audio:	Shot:
	Location:

Form 4.1 Storyboarding template

Scriptwriting

Having students write scripts comes next. I don't teach screenwriting and wouldn't recommend spending the time to teach and evaluate scriptwriting techniques unless that's one of your curricular goals. I do have students write their scripts in a word processing document using a two-column table (Form 4.2). On the left column of the table students include all audio. On the right, students include the shot, location, and a description of what the viewers will see.

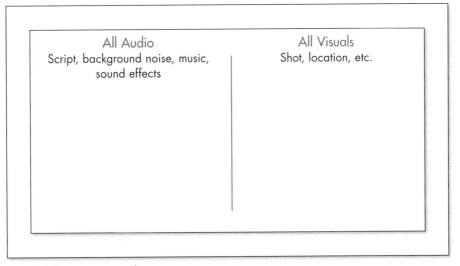

Form 4.2 Scriptwriting template

After the first draft of the script is complete, I provide a handout to help students learn how to "peer edit." The peer-editing guides I use are very similar to what I would use if students were editing one another's essays. Here is a peer-editing tool you can view online:

> **Script evaluation tool:** www.teachwithvideo.com/download_archives/Sports_ Skill_Peer_Resp.pdf

Students evaluate scripts based on the rubric. Student editors give suggestions to the authors for improvement and also point out strong components. After peer editing, I have them discuss suggested changes, then the author writes the second draft. I review the second draft, also using the peer-editing guide. The authors make adjustments to the script based on my assessment and feedback. When the next draft of the script is ready, I review it again and either approve the script or have the writer make more adjustments. We repeat this process until the script is approved.

If we are working on a group project, I assign the students to specific groups, then we read all of the scripts and decide which one each group will turn into a movie. Each student will be given a specific role and responsibilities in the production. I provide a "Movie Jobs Description" handout for this.

> **Movie jobs description handout:** www.teachwithvideo.com/download_archives/History_Job_Desc.pdf

Setting the Stage

Now, students prepare any needed costumes, props, and sets. I don't ask them to build anything, just to put in some effort to make the movie look more authentic. Props include any physical objects necessary to tell the story. Costumes may include appropriate attire, such as hockey gear to demonstrate a slap shot, or a lab coat and goggles for a science experiment. Students making a historical drama should dress to look like their characters. I require students to research clothing appropriate to the time period, and base their costumes on a specific image they've found of the period's clothing. I ask students to be creative and thrifty in making these costumes, doing their best to have an authentic look while spending little or no money. Some examples of costumes my students have created can be seen at www.stevenkatz.com/student-work/us-history-videos/.

Rehearsing, Shooting, and Publishing

Rehearsing

When I first began doing movie projects with students, I didn't dedicate time for rehearsal, but I found that students often forgot about the script and just ad-libbed. Rehearsal gives students the opportunity to practice their lines and all other aspects of the script before filming. I usually dedicate an entire class period to rehearsal, having students pretend they are working in front of the camera. This results in a better quality movie, and students can take advantage of more time for planning and writing.

Shooting

After rehearsal and before filming, we discuss filming techniques to help students produce a watchable movie. I discuss simple, common sense ideas such as using a tripod, making sure there's enough light, and filming in a quiet place. I also explain how to get what they have filmed from the camera into the computer.

Evaluating and Publishing

After the first day of filming, I give a tutorial on the editing software. I show how to select, trim, and move clips; how to add titles and transitions; and how to manipulate sound. When students are ready to finish the editing, I show them how to export and publish the movie.

Before students publish their movies I like to spend some time having groups evaluate each other's work. I have them use a rubric to evaluate the movies, adding suggestions for improvement. In addition, I also have each group do a self-evaluation of their movie.

If possible, I try to organize a school assembly to show the movies my students have completed. At the very least, I show all of the movies to the classes who created them. I think it's important for students to get recognition on campus for the work they've done. The impact on the school can often go beyond showing the movies. I've witnessed many students become on-campus celebrities.

Distributing the movies publicly can be a little trickier. If you plan to display student work online, it's important that parents have signed release forms and that the students (and you) have followed all copyright laws and have provided credit to sources in order to protect your school and your students. Posting videos to YouTube or Vimeo is one way to publish; both of these sites have privacy options so that movies can only be seen by designated people. Another option is to post the movies to a blog that has privacy protection, and provide the password to people who are allowed to view the video. You can also save the movie onto a CD, DVD, or flash drive, although as internet speed continues to increase these options are becoming less popular.

One other way of students being recognized for the work they've done is to enter them into a movie competition or multimedia festival. There are many worldwide, and some even offer prizes to the winners. You can find contests to enter on the web-based resource Online Video Contests (www.onlinevideocontests.com).

With parental permission, I have included various examples of my students' movies on my website Steven Katz: Empowering Teachers & Students (www. stevenkatz.com).

Standards Addressed

Moviemaking can be used in a wide range of grades. If the activity is done in Grade 6, these Common Core ELA Literacy Standards would be met:

Common Core State Standards

Grade 6 Writing

W.6.1   Write arguments to support claims with clear reasons and relevant evidence.

W.6.2   Write informative/explanatory texts to examine a topic and convey ideas, concepts, and information through the selection, organization, and analysis of relevant content.

W.6.3   Write narratives to develop real or imagined experiences or events using effective technique, relevant descriptive details, and well-structured event sequences.

W.6.4   Produce clear and coherent writing in which the development, organization, and style are appropriate to task, purpose, and audience.

W.6.5   With some guidance and support from peers and adults, develop and strengthen writing as needed by planning, revising, editing, rewriting, or trying a new approach. (Editing for conventions should demonstrate command of Language standards 1–3 up to and including grade 6.)

W.6.8   Gather relevant information from multiple print and digital sources; assess the credibility of each source; and quote or paraphrase the data and conclusions of others while avoiding plagiarism and providing basic bibliographic information for sources.

W.6.10 Write routinely over extended time frames (time for research, reflection, and revision) and shorter time frames (a single sitting or a day or two) for a range of discipline-specific tasks, purposes, and audiences.

Grade 6 Speaking and Listening

SL.6.1   Engage effectively in a range of collaborative discussions (one-on-one, in groups, and teacher-led) with diverse partners on grade 6 topics, texts, and issues, building on others' ideas and expressing their own clearly.

SL.6.4   Present claims and findings, sequencing ideas logically and using pertinent descriptions, facts, and details to accentuate main ideas or themes; use appropriate eye contact, adequate volume, and clear pronunciation.

SL.6.5   Include multimedia components (e.g., graphics, images, music, sound) and visual displays in presentations to clarify information.

Grade 6 Language

L.6.1   Demonstrate command of the conventions of standard English grammar and usage when writing or speaking.

L.6.3   Use knowledge of language and its conventions when writing, speaking, reading, or listening.

L.6.6   Acquire and use accurately grade-appropriate general academic and domain-specific words and phrases; gather vocabulary knowledge when considering a word or phrase important to comprehension or expression.

Grade 4

The Grade 6 CCSS given here are very similar to upper elementary standards and high school grade standards. If the activity is done in Grade 4, here are the Common Core State Standards for ELA Literacy that would be met for Grade 4 in Writing (www.corestandards.org/ELA-Literacy/W/4), Speaking and Listening (www.corestandards.org/ELA-Literacy/SL/4), and Language (www.corestandards.org/ELA-Literacy/L/4):

- W.4.1, W.4.2, W.4.3, W.4.4, W.4.5, W.4.8, and W.4.10

- SL.4.1, SL.4.4, and SL.4.5

- L.4.1, L.4.3, and L.4.6

Grades 9–10

If the activity is done in high school, here are the Common Core ELA Literacy Standards that would be met for Grades 9–10 in Writing (www.corestandards. org/ELA-Literacy/W/9-10), Speaking and Listening (www.corestandards. org/ELA-Literacy/SL/9-10), and Language (www.corestandards.org/ ELA-Literacy/L/9-10):

- W.9–10.1, W.9–10.2, W.9–10.3, W.9–10.4, W.9–10.5, W.9–10.6, W.9–10.8, and W.9–10.10

- SL.9–10.1, SL.9–10.4, and SL.9–10.5

- L.9–10.1, L.9–10.3, and L.9–10.6

While student video projects described in this chapter may relate to a broad array of the CCSS, the above are standards for which there is a particularly clear and strong connection.

CHAPTER 5

Do-It-Yourself Digital 3D Storytelling

Jennifer Latimer

LEVEL

Grades 3–12 / Ages 7–18 / Elementary, Middle, and High School

TECHNOLOGIES

PowerPoint, microphone, digital camera, Soungle

LITERACY

Digital storytelling, including text, sound effects, and visuals

STANDARDS

ISTE Standards•S, AASL, CCSS for ELA (Speaking and Listening, *SL*)

D o-It-Yourself Digital Storytelling in Three Dimensions (Do-It-Yourself Digital 3D Storytelling, DIY3D) is a storytelling format that allows students to combine elements of modern media culture with three storytelling dimensions—words, art, and sound—to craft their own lively stories. In this project, students create original stories in a six-week participatory learning project using PowerPoint, with the option to convert the stories to movie files viewable in Apple QuickTime or Windows Media Center. They tell the story in three minutes with five frames and 50 words. Students engage with current media while learning key skills such as ethical use of other people's media (intellectual property), collaboration, creativity, fluency, and media literacy. DIY3D reflects the Common Core ELA standards of Speaking and Listening: Presentation of Knowledge and Ideas, as well as the ISTE Standards·S of creativity, innovation, and digital citizenship.

Background

Clinton Elementary School in Maplewood, New Jersey, is a K–5 elementary school in the South Orange/Maplewood School District. We have a diverse student population representing 25 countries of origin and a broad socioeconomic range. The DIY3D storytelling approach resulted from our search for a literacy-based project aligned with our school's vision statement:

> Based on the core belief that all students have the ability to learn, all members of the Clinton School community will empower each child to reach his or her fullest potential.
>
> As lifelong learners, our students will possess core academic knowledge and 21st-century skills leading them to become respectful, accepting, productive, and responsible citizens in this global society.

With the full support and encouragement of the school principal, the DIY3D program was created for our third grade. This long-term and low-cost program was aligned with our curriculum and philosophies of teaching and learning. Our school library media center was the perfect venue to provide a foundation for all students to engage in a high-level creative endeavor such as DIY3D. Posters prominently displayed in the library announced many of our important goals for students, such as our desire for them to read, write, learn, create, and grow.

Keys to Project Success

In this project, students choose one of six images to be the centerpiece of an original multimedia story. They tell the story with five frames of photos, 50 words, and within a time frame of three minutes. Their final digital stories are shared in the classroom and then unveiled in the auditorium to an audience of their student peers, their families, and other school classes.

Students have the opportunity to work in small groups over a six-week period with a clear project scope. Flexibility and creative choice allow students to develop storylines of personal interest. The project is differentiated so that all students can work at their own level. Storytelling using our three dimensions—words, art, and sound—allows all students to take an active role, using one or all of the dimensions. The project was made available to the entire third grade due to the minimal cost involved. This approach can be adapted for implementation in Grades 3–12.

Project Dimensions

This project encourages the students to collaborate in small groups (three to four students) to create an original story based on a single image chosen by group consensus. Students edit the narration to 50 words or fewer (40 minimum, 50 maximum). The limited length challenges students to make certain that all three dimensions support the story. Original art is created and sound effects are chosen effectively and ethically to support the plot line. Finished stories are prepared in PowerPoint, challenging students to apply presentation skills such as emphasis, clarity, and tone.

Time Allowance

For this project we allow one hour per week for six weeks.

Design and Plan the Project

The project was conceived to be implemented by the classroom teacher with the support of the library/media specialist, the art teacher, and parents and volunteers.

Several weeks before the proposed start of the project, we set aside planning time for the teachers. Parents/volunteers will also need some planning time.

The classroom teacher should meet with the technology coordinator or library media center specialist to

- determine the classroom curriculum goals and expectations. (Our students were focused on writing narrative fiction and applying the editing process to their works.)

- discuss individual student needs.

The classroom teacher should also meet with the school art teacher to

- secure support of project and availability of classroom time.

- determine appropriate art supplies that will be used to address the needs and skills of all students. This might include paper, pencils, markers, crayons, and magazine pictures.

- plan for additional time to share student rough drafts so that the art teacher may assist in providing ideas for the visual representation of the text.

Resources Needed

In addition to art supplies mentioned above, the teacher will need

- at least one computer with Microsoft PowerPoint, a microphone, and a digital camera.

- a laptop, while not essential, allows students to play the sound effects outside of PowerPoint. Sound effects essentially serve as additional "voices" in the recording to help tell the story.

- images to use as story starters.

- sound effects to support the student's stories, which can be downloaded royalty free at the Soungle website (www.soungle.com).

Procedures

Week One: Working on Words

One of the goals of the DIY3D project is for students to understand and demonstrate the subtleties of language and how our manner of speaking impacts the words we speak or write. To warm up the class, use the "O" activity, which is based on the work of Christopher Shamburg (Shamburg, 2012). "O" is a great letter and word in the English language that can be used to help students learn about expression and delivery. Show them the letter "O" on the board and have them say the letter after you provide various situations for them:

- They are sad …

- They are angry …

- They are surprised …

- They stubbed their toe …

- They won the lottery …

Briefly discuss with students how "O" and "Oh" can have multiple meanings by simply changing the framing of the situation in which it is used.

Next, complete the "I didn't say he ate your sandwich" activity. Ask students to repeat that line, but place the accent on different words. It is helpful to have the sentences displayed for students to read as they are doing the activity. Highlight or underline different words each time as shown below:

- **I** didn't say he ate your sandwich.

- I didn't **say** he ate your sandwich.

- I didn't say **he** ate your sandwich.

- I didn't say he **ate** your sandwich.

- I didn't say he ate **your** sandwich.

- I didn't say he ate your **sandwich**.

Ask students to explain what is happening in each scenario depending on which words are emphasized.

Week One: Working on Sounds

For your final activity on the first day, have students individually or in small groups create two-line sentences based on sounds. Select sounds such as an engine racing, a phone ringing, water splashing, a heart beating, and crickets chirping. Sound examples can be created or found at the Soungle website. Students listen to the sounds and use the sounds to help them write sentences.

For example, play a heartbeat and show the sentences, "One day I woke up late for school. I ran down the street so that I would not miss the bus." The students can then read their lines and play their chosen sound effect for the class to hear it. Discuss how the sound effect can help tell the story, move action forward, create a feeling, or engage the reader without specific references or explanation.

Week Two: Introducing a Central Image

Assign students to teams of three or four. At this point there are two approaches that may be used. The first is to provide each group with a selection of action-based images familiar to the students. This approach is based on the popularity of fan fiction and the belief that students can be inspired by stories and images they know and still create original works. For this project we used images from Jeff Kinney's *Diary of a Wimpy Kid;* Dav Pilkey's *Captain Underpants; Snow White* by the Brothers Grimm; and Grant Morrison's *Batman and Robin,* in addition to paintings by Degas and Kandinsky. At this point we discuss the ethical considerations of using other people's work. I give a short overview of copyright law as well as fair use, in developmentally appropriate language. We discuss the differences between copying without permission and using someone else's work to create transformative and original works.

If time does not warrant engagement with the ethical consideration of images, the second approach is to provide students with common images or clip art that show action, such as children or animals in motion. The action will assist students in telling what happened before and after the image.

Students collaborate and choose an image for their story. Their chosen image is glued to a 4 × 6-inch card and becomes the middle page of the story they are about to create, in which they will tell what happened before, during, and after their image (Figure 5.1). Students will have the opportunity to create the first two and last two images of the story themselves in a later week (Figure 5.8). The goal is to limit the story to five images, up to four sounds, and 40–50 words.

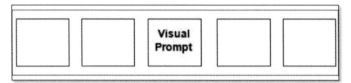

Figure 5.1 Student-chosen visual prompt becomes the third image in the sequence of five.

Week Three: Developing the Story, Sketches, and Script

Students write and edit stories (Figure 5.2) as well as sketch pictures (Figure 5.3) for their pages based around their chosen visual image so that they meet the goal of 40–50 words. Group members may opt to write scenes or sketch pictures in whatever order they choose. This option allows visual thinkers to see the scene unfold visually and then focus on the dialogue. As the storyline develops, students choose the types of sounds they want to use to support each of their five pages. Lastly, as the story unfolds, students create a script for the story in which each group member is included and reads a portion of the script (Figure 5.4).

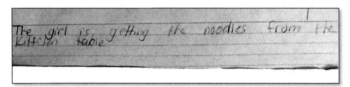

Figure 5.2 Students create narration on the back of a 4 × 6-inch card.

Figure 5.3 Students create pencil sketches on the front of a 4 × 6-inch card.

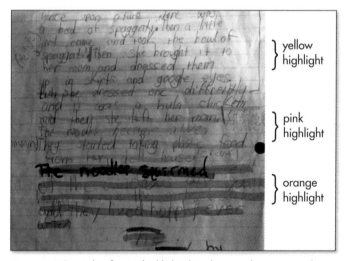

Figure 5.4 Example of script highlighted to show each group member's lines (yellow highlight at top, pink in middle, and orange at bottom).

It is important that the teacher model visual and sound dimensions. In this way, students will see that their images and sound choices can replace words and demonstrate action in the story.

For example, in Figure 5.5 too many words are used.

Figure 5.5 Original version uses only art and words (too many words) to illustrate story.

"Late one night" can be removed since the picture represents that it is night and instead of saying "the phone rang," students will insert a sound effect of a phone ringing (Figure 5.6).

Figure 5.6 Setting speaks for itself (late at night). And so does the phone (ringing).

Finally, the description of Melissa as "half asleep" can be replaced by a student saying "Hello" in a sleepy voice (Figure 5.7).

Figure 5.7 Final version replaces "Melissa was half asleep" with a sleepy-voice delivery.

Students will see that there are many ways to convey meaning beyond the written word.

Week Four: Working on Images and Sounds

In art class, students will create the final background imagery for the stories, based on their sketches. The art teacher provides a variety of materials such as paint, pencils, pens, and magazines. Students can illustrate or make their scenes using magazines or other pictures. In Figure 5.8, the students used colored pencils to illustrate frames #1, #2, #4, and #5. Groups choose sounds after a discussion on the ethical use of sounds.

Figure 5.8 An example of a finished five-part student story

Week Five/Six: Finalizing Words, Art, and Sound

Before class, take digital photos of the four student-created drawings and upload them into students' PowerPoint presentations as frames #1, #2, #4, and #5, alongside the initial visual prompt chosen by the group (frame #3). Converting drawings to PowerPoint images by using a digital photo is artistically liberating for students who are challenged by creating images in a computer program. Jeff Share developed this process as a practical application of his "Critical Media Literacy" in elementary classrooms (Share, 2008).

One PowerPoint file per class is recommended if you are completing this project with multiple classes. This allows the file size to remain manageable and easier to share. Our projects contained an opening slide with the classroom teacher's name, an introduction slide containing the group's number and each group's five slides. An example PowerPoint presentation for a class of 20 students (five groups of four students each) would have approximately 31 slides.

Students record the audio of their stories into PowerPoint one page at a time, taking care to apply their skills of emphasis, clarity, and tone. Depending on the version of PowerPoint available, this function may be labeled as "Record Narration," "Record Audio," or a similar name.

Assessment and Standards Addressed

Assessment

When we assess the third grade projects, we use a rubric that considers the learning factors of audience response, techniques, and group work. We also rate the projects as exemplary, satisfactory, or work in progress (Table 5.1). This rubric could be adapted for other learning factors and grade levels.

Table 5.1 Sample Assessment Rubric

CATEGORY	Exemplary	Satisfactory	Work in progress
Audience response	Final story is engaging for audience regardless of their familiarity with the source image.	Final story is engaging for some members of audience depending on their prior knowledge of source image.	Final story is not complete and needs additional assistance.
Techniques	Audio recording, art, and sound support the story.	Audio recording, art, and sound generally support the story.	Audio recording, art, and sound do not support the story.
Group work	All members clearly participated in the creation and presentation.	Some of the students participated in the creation and presentation.	The group needs assistance in working on collaboration.

Standards Addressed

This project addresses the ISTE Standards•S (Appendix, www.iste.org/standards/standards-for-students); American Association of School Librarians (AASL) Standards for the 21st Century Learner (www.ala.org/aasl/standards-guidelines/learning-standards); and Common Core State Standards for English Language Arts, Grade 3, Speaking and Listening (www.corestandards.org/ELA-Literacy/SL/3).

Table 5.2 Standards Addressed

CATEGORY	Related ISTE Standards•S	Related AASL standards	Common Core ELA standards
Audience response	1.a, 1.b, 3.b	2.1.6, 3.1.3, 4.1.3	CC.3.SL.5
Techniques	1.a, 1.b, 6.a, 6.b, 6.d	1.2.3, 2.1.6, 4.1.3	CC.3.SL.5
Legal and ethical guidelines	5.a, 6.a	1.3.1, 1.3.3, 1.3.5, 3.1.6, 4.3.4	

Concluding Thoughts

Please note that this lesson was designed for our third grade students, many of whom needed assistance throughout the design and creation process. Other grades and populations of students

- may not need a visual prompt and may have the ability to choose an appropriate image independently;

- may photograph art and upload into PowerPoint without teacher assistance;

- may choose to create their own sound effects using their voice, musical instruments, or household objects; and

- may choose to use multiple languages.

Many students have the ability to work creatively and independently and can be offered more freedom to choose appropriate dimensions. This project can also be expanded to include concepts or readings beyond fiction. Students might be tasked to teach a concept to other students. One of our second grade classes created a presentation about shadows. Students created word clouds, original poetry, and stories taking on the voice of a shadow as a teaching tool for themselves and other classes, all using our DIY3D approach.

You will find an overview of the DIY3D project on my website, the Anywhere Librarian (www.anywherelibrarian.com/?page_id=387).

References

American Association of School Librarians. (2007). *Standards for the 21st-century learner.* Chicago, IL: Author. Retrieved from www.ala.org/aasl/standards-guidelines/learning-standards

Clinton Elementary School. (2013) Vision statement. Retrieved from www.clintonelementary.org/about-clinton-elementary/prinicpals-message/

International Society for Technology in Education (ISTE). (2007). *National educational technology standards for students (NETS·S)* (2nd ed.). Eugene, OR: Author. Retrieved from www.iste.org/standards/nets-for-students

National Governors Association Center for Best Practices, Council of Chief State School Officers. (2010). *Common Core State Standards for English language arts & literacy.* Washington, DC: National Governors Association Center for Best Practices. Retrieved from www.corestandards.org/the-standards

Shamburg, C. (2012). From O to the big ideas in ed tech. Retrieved from www.slideshare.net/cs272/kenilworth-pd-big-ideas-in-ed-tech

Share, J. (2008). *Media literacy is elementary.* New York, NY: Peter Lang.

SECTION II

ANALYZING AND
discussing literature

CHAPTER 6

Online Literature Circles, Quick Writes, and More
  Grade 8 / Ages 13–14 / Middle School
  Edmodo, Ning, CoveritLive, TodaysMeet

CHAPTER 7

Honoring Student Voice Through Blogging
  Grade 6 / Ages 11–12 / Middle School
  Blogging platforms: 21Classes, Weebly

Online Literature Circles, Quick Writes, and More

Debbie Shoulders

LEVEL

Grade 8 / Ages 13–14 / Middle School

TECHNOLOGIES

Edmodo, Ning, CoveritLive, TodaysMeet

LITERACY

Literature circles

STANDARDS

ISTE Standards•S, Common Core ELA (Speaking and Listening, *SL*)

S tudents chattering in the hallways on the way to class, gossiping over lunch, and laughing together on the way to the buses: These are scenes that take place every day during school. When many of those same students enter a classroom, that eagerness diminishes. A few individuals will volunteer to respond to a question, but lively on-task conversations from all learners are rare. Sound familiar? Such was the case with my eighth grade English language arts students.

Many years ago, my main form of communication with friends was via telephone, or a weekly visit in person. Nowadays, the in-person visit happens perhaps once a month, and I am rarely on the phone. Even so, I know more than ever about what is happening within my circle of friends and acquaintances, through social networking media like Facebook, Pinterest, Plurk, and Twitter. What's more, I enjoy the time I spend perusing these sites!

This started me thinking: My communication methods are similar to my teen students'. What if I brought social networking tools into an educational setting? Would I see a positive shift in student attitudes and learning if the learning environment mirrored their socially networked world?

Putting the Idea to Work

Although I've taught several content areas during my career, I've always based instruction on literacy: the ability to communicate through reading, writing, and speaking. Since the 1990s when I began using an Apple IIe, I've also worked at integrating technology into the curriculum, seeing potential for the tools to motivate students and make tasks easier. Combining these two important ideas, literacy and technology, has guided my planning, instruction, and assessment. It's the context I see for the use of social networking, as a tool to increase students' ability to comprehend texts, to improve analytical discussions, and help students to write effectively.

My initial attempt in implementing this concept was through the use of Thinkquest, a "gated" community for K–12 students and teachers. It was considered gated because teachers had to apply for membership, and only students admitted by teachers could participate. Despite the somewhat childish background and avatars, my students were thrilled with the use of Thinkquest. They loved having their own web page to share ideas and interests, and I loved having the ability to communicate with students after school hours. My biggest challenge was teaching copyright and fair use policies and making sure these rules were followed. It is very easy to "grab" what you want on the internet to decorate a web page.

As my confidence grew, I found Thinkquest to be too confining for my needs and discovered Edmodo. (That's fortunate, because Thinkquest had decided to drop this component of its platform.) Edmodo includes most of the tools necessary to encourage communication and social interaction, and it is also free. Edmodo is gated as well, in that you choose who can join your group by supplying a code. But it does allow individuals beyond the school community—such as authors—to join groups, making it a way to communicate with content experts.

Literacy Applications

Of course it is not just the tool, but the way it's used for instruction that determines academic success. I began using Edmodo as a place to do simple "quick writes": I post an open-ended question about the anchor book students read during a particular unit, and students must post one response to the question and two comments about other postings (Figure 6.1). This is a quick way to determine comprehension for all of the students before continuing the next day's reading. While I often discover misunderstandings through the added comments, peers will also see them and attempt to set their classmates straight.

Figure 6.1 Student discussion in Edmodo

I recently used the "Award Badge" feature that Edmodo includes, designing a badge to recognize a "Thoughtful Thinker" for the quick writes. These assignments can become routine, so I was looking for a way to motivate students to go beyond the obvious. My eighth graders now come to class ready to see if their response earned an award.

Success in the use of discussion boards in general requires a conversation with students about netiquette, the proper way to behave with online communication. You don't want any student to feel uncomfortable because of a comment made by a fellow student. I'm hoping that Edmodo will improve their site's options for threaded discussions, which would make the reading of a long discussion easier.

Literature Circles and More

Literature Circles with Ning

It is important for me to have two particular functions—threaded discussions and groups—in order to conduct online literature circles, and one social networking site that allows for threaded discussions is Ning. Ning looks and performs somewhat like Facebook. Ning users must pay a fee and there are a variety of price levels, depending on which options the user (e.g., teacher or school) chooses. At present time, to have the ability to form groups, the cost is about $200 a year.

For my literature circles, several times a year students choose similar books or books of similar genres, and form groups. They meet about once a week at Ning to discuss their interpretations of the readings (Figure 6.2).

Literature circles at Ning became a wonderful addition to my ELA curriculum. Rather than run from group to group to assess participation and understanding, I can actually "pop in" during a group's discussion, then later I can look at what actually took place. Again, all students are engaged in the communication, albeit in small discussion groups. Students also don't seem to sense my presence and feel free to be themselves, so I may glimpse another aspect of their personalities not evident in face-to-face discussions. For example, during one such discussion, a student unjustly blamed me for his lack of preparation for the meeting. His peers quickly came to my defense, pointing out to him wiser alternatives to the actions he chose. While it was bit off-topic, their advice allowed the group's conversation to get back on track and meet the instructional goal for that day.

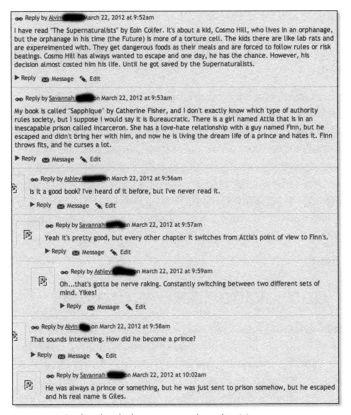

Figure 6.2 Student book discussion conducted in Ning

Real-time Discussions with CoveritLive and TodaysMeet

Impressed by my initial success with gathering responses from all of my students and sensing their level of motivation, I decided to try a whole-class, real-time book discussion using an online tool. Two free web resources met my requirements for this: CoveritLive (www.coveritlive.com) and TodaysMeet (www.todaysmeet.com). CoveritLive requires a login and some preparation. It must be embedded into a wiki, blog, or website, but it does allow private monitoring of comments during the discussion. This helps to avoid off-task behaviors. TodaysMeet can be set up in minutes, requires no login, and anyone can participate as long as they have the URL. There are no private monitoring features.

I have used the online discussion format as a modified Socratic seminar, where everyone asks questions about literature and responds to other participants. I participate as well. This does take some quick observation and keyboarding skills, but these can improve with practice.

Class discussions with a content expert are another way to use online synchronized meeting places. I have found that some "experts" are shy about videoconferencing; they prefer this method of communication. A retired principal who took on this role found that my students are passionate about their causes, and she had to defend such policies as dress codes and eating in the classrooms. Despite the differing views, the students had a quality primary source for their research papers on the same issues. With this method, all students participate, whereas with video or audio conferencing, one student at a time asks a question or poses a response while the remainder of the class observes.

Assessment and Standards Addressed

Participation in instructional social networking experiences is mandatory in my class. I will allow shy students to opt out of facing an entire class, but the relative anonymity of the online experience means: "You must participate!" To help make students accountable, the activities are assessed. I have found rubrics to be the best way to evaluate this practice, often utilizing Rubistar (http://rubistar4teachers.org), a free online rubric creator, to make them (Figures 6.3 and 6.4). The rubrics are available to students through the class wiki—before and during any activity or project—so they know what to expect. I am particularly concerned about such performance elements as frequent contributions, on-task conversations, and defending ideas with references to the texts involved. Therefore, the assessment is not only participation, but participation that contributes to useful and insightful ideas.

Literature Circle Rubric   ☆   📄 Edit

Collaborative Work Skills : Literature Circles

Teacher Name: **Mrs. Shoulders**

Student Name: _____

CATEGORY	4	3	2	1
Contributions	Routinely provides useful ideas when participating in the group and in classroom discussion. A definite leader who contributes a lot of effort.	Usually provides useful ideas when participating in the group and in classroom discussion. A strong group member who tries hard!	Sometimes provides useful ideas when participating in the group and in classroom discussion. A satisfactory group member who does what is required.	Rarely provides useful ideas when participating in the group and in classroom discussion. May refuse to participate.
Quality of Work	Provides work of the highest quality.	Provides high quality work.	Provides work that occasionally needs to be checked/redone by other group members to ensure quality.	Provides work that usually needs to be checked/redone by others to ensure quality.
Focus on the task	Consistently stays focused on the task and what needs to be done. Very self-directed.	Focuses on the task and what needs to be done most of the time. Other group members can count on this person.	Focuses on the task and what needs to be done some of the time. Other group members must sometimes nag, prod, and remind to keep this person on-task.	Rarely focuses on the task and what needs to be done. Lets others do the work.
Monitors Group Effectiveness	Routinely monitors the effectiveness of the group, and makes suggestions to make it more effective.	Routinely monitors the effectiveness of the group and works to make the group more effective.	Occasionally monitors the effectiveness of the group and works to make the group more effective.	Rarely monitors the effectiveness of the group and does not work to make it more effective.

Figure 6.3 Rubistar-created rubric

☆ Blogging Rubric   ☐ Edit

First Semester Blogging Rubric

Literature Blog Scoring Guide		
Name:		Date:
Performance Element	**Value**	**Your Score**
Wrote the assigned _____ blog entries.	20	
Used the prompt to guide discussion by referring to story elements and personal experiences.	20	
Use examples from the book to defend ideas.	20	
Wrote in complete sentences that demonstrated grammar, capitalization, and punctuation rules.	20	
Blog included a heading that was the title of the book, the date, and was published.	20	
	Total Score	

Figure 6.4 Teacher-created rubric

ISTE Standards•S

So how does all this fit in with the standards? ISTE Standards for Students (Appendix) has an entire section dedicated to Communication and Collaboration. Part of the expectation is that students "interact, collaborate, and publish with peers, experts, or others employing a variety of digital environments and media." Students tend to be social by nature. The challenge, then, becomes how to create authentic instructional experiences that reflect this. The quick writes and literature circles help with the analytic skills necessary for reading comprehension, but are used in a setting that appeals to the teen personality.

A benefit of collaboration is the sharing of information, and that sharing is carried out in the teen vernacular. Through online communication, peers help peers. The information is archived for later use. If a student is absent, he can participate from home, keeping abreast of daily instructional goals. In this way, learning and school extend beyond the walls of the classroom. I no longer feel the stress of trying to "get it all in" during a 45-minute lesson.

Common Core ELA Standards

The Common Core Standards for ELA (Speaking and Listening) include the idea of "engaging effectively in a range of collaborative discussions." Students come to these discussions prepared, having read or researched material under study. To be successful in quick writes, literature circles, class discussions, or blogging, learners must have those skills. Neither the discussion nor the tool is the learning; it is the preparation beforehand that enables students to analyze and synthesize their ideas. My students know what is required of them before they engage in any online collaborative effort.

Conclusion

I teach in an ideal situation. Discovering my passion for books, I was transferred from my position as a computer technology teacher to the ELA department but was allowed to stay in my computer lab. While this definitely makes things easier for me, the rest of the staff has access to seven shared mobile labs. Those teachers who see the need for using technology use tools like the ones I describe, often. It just takes a little planning and ingenuity on their part. It's important that school districts understand the need for students to read and write with the tools that are part of their daily lives; computers must be part of every child's educational experience in order to accomplish this. I also hope that teachers realize that students need to interact while learning. Social networking offers an engaging and effective way to meet those needs.

Resources

CoveritLive: www.coveritlive.com

Edmodo: www.edmodo.com

Ning: www.ning.com

Rubistar: http://rubistar.4teachers.org

Thinkquest: www.thinkquest.org

TodaysMeet: www.todaysmeet.com

CHAPTER 7

Honoring Student Voice Through Blogging

Mary Paulson and Leah Larson

LEVEL

Grade 6 / Ages 11–12 / Middle School

TECHNOLOGY

Blogging platforms: 21Classes, Weebly

LITERACY

Discussions of literature

STANDARDS

ISTE Standards•S, CCSS for ELA (Reading: Literature, *RL*)

As is true for many teachers throughout the country, Mary Paulson continually reflects on her practice, keeping one eye on the achievement gap and the other on state mandated standards, while maintaining high expectations for all students.

Teaching in a school with a culturally diverse student population presents another set of challenges. Research tells us that when students see themselves in text, they engage more fully in study activities—but how could she motivate students who were hesitant to participate? Although not particularly tech savvy, she was certain that technology could facilitate multiple instructional components of their book study. Media specialist Leah Larson stepped in to give a helping hand with the technology.

Background

Paulson is a sixth grade language arts teacher in an urban school district in Golden Valley, Minnesota. The student demographic is diverse: Native American 2%, Asian 7%, Hispanic 40%, African American 23%, and White 28%. The sixth graders are divided into teams, each handled by three or four teachers. In order to problem solve around district goals, each department meets monthly as a school improvement goal group to reflect on strategies that work in the classroom.

Some time ago, our Language Arts (LA) Department decided to add culturally relevant material to the curriculum. Consequently, Paulson's sixth grade LA team decided to purchase the adventure novel *Crossing the Wire* by Will Hobbs for our novel study unit. The team felt the choice moved us forward in adding culturally relevant material to the curriculum.

The adventure novel *Crossing the Wire* is about a boy who crosses the border illegally from Mexico into the United States. It's a fast-paced book that includes many universal themes. Those themes—immigration, belonging, freedom, and survival—thread their way in and out of the book.

The specific English language arts standards the team intended to address in our book study include describing how a particular story or drama plot unfolds in a series of episodes that include character change, citing textual evidence to support analysis of text as well as determining theme through particular details, determining theme and how it is supported through details, and inferencing.

Inferencing is an important cognitive skill that involves the use of background knowledge and information from the text to develop a plausible conclusion.

Another goal was to activate prior knowledge surrounding immigration that could provide for rich discussion, allowing all students to participate, including hesitant students. With our high number of Hispanic students, many of whom hesitate to participate, we hoped some would have personal stories to tell or connections that could be made to the topic of immigration.

Ideas were circling in Paulson's head when she tapped the expertise of media specialist Leah Larson. Larson liked the idea of a blog as a way to meet some of the technology standards recently embedded in the language arts curriculum. Also, Paulson wanted to change the form of discussions so students with personal connections to immigration could participate in a nonthreatening way, honoring all voices. In the past, there was a pattern of the same students participating in discussions continually, while some didn't join in at all. Some students who usually didn't participate might bring a different perspective because of different background experiences. It was important to somehow include their voices, as well.

Beginning Our Blogging Journey

Larson and Paulson met to do some preliminary planning and crafted a blogging activity that would activate prior student knowledge. To begin, we read the first two chapters of the book to gain some background knowledge, then Paulson used her classroom computer and interactive whiteboard to demonstrate how to access the blogging resource. She also provided students with these instructions in a hard copy handout. Finally, she assigned questions in her own teacher blog post for the students to answer.

The questions posted included:

1. If you were a friend of Victor's, what advice would you give him as he prepares to cross the wire?

2. If you were Victor, would you cross the wire?

3. If you had to cross the wire, what would you pack for the journey?

These questions are meant to engage students in higher-order thinking as they make predictions, synthesize information, and activate background knowledge.

Next, she reserved the computer lab for two days in a row, and planned student activities for those days. She planned a two-step process in order to have students set up their blogs one day and the next day move on to answering the posted questions.

On the first day in the computer lab, students set up their blogs by choosing a banner (background picture) and title and following directions in order to publish it. If they had time left, students were to begin writing a response to the three questions posted on the teacher's blog. She also posted the questions in large-format hard copy in the computer lab. That way, students would not waste time going back and forth between having to read the questions on the teacher's blog and then returning to their own blog in order to post their responses.

The following day in the computer lab, she prepped the students so they could begin posting comments on one another's blogs.

As the blogging began, there was a buzz in the room. Students realized how quickly they could send a comment to another student in the class. Blogging, my students had figured out, was the next best thing to texting. The thrill of partici-pating in social media was contagious. She encouraged students to write responses that included details and evidence from the text and also checked for complete sentences, grammar, and correct spelling. (Save the texting lingo for cell phones!)

During this intense interchange of postings, it became apparent that the playing field had been leveled. Students who rarely raised their hand to participate during class were posting well-developed comments and challenging classmates with questions of their own. We were honoring student voices! The teacher didn't say a thing to them except for an occasional comment. Students learned from each other and realized how diversity can be celebrated. The thinking process of comparing personal responses with students who have different background experiences promoted comparing, contrasting, and then clarifying to support understanding. Truly, it was a celebration of diversity!

Suddenly the class was over, and students were reluctant to stop posting comments. For the first time ever, students did not remind me that it was time for lunch. The level of engagement exceeded teacher expectations. Clearly, even though setting up blogs takes some preparation, in the end, the students' responses made it clear that it was worth it.

How to Set Up Blogs

For an experience like the one described, teachers and students need regular access to computers with internet capabilities. An LCD projector is useful for demonstrating the blogging process to students and displaying the teacher blog. The project also requires a blogging platform (resource), preferably one designed for educational use with a variety of security settings.

1. Select a blogging platform for your project. For this project, we successfully used 21Classes (www.21classes.com) and Weebly (www.weebly.com). Both offer free or low-cost educational options, as well as teacher control over student comments and settings to protect student safety.

2. Create your own teacher blog. This will familiarize you with the platform and walk you through the same process that students will use to create their own blogs.

3. Make sure student blogs and safety settings reflect your school's electronic use policies. Leave plenty of time for this step, as the process can be time consuming.

4. Create a centralized site from which students can easily access their own—and one another's—blogs. Some platforms provide this service automatically. (We have also created such a site as part of our school's web page or the teacher's blog.)

5. Create a presentation and handout to walk students through the process of creating their own blogs. We typically demonstrate this for students in the computer lab so they are able to apply the steps immediately. The handout can be used as a reference.

6. Manage student blog creation. The teacher typically checks student blogs daily for the first two to three days that students work on their projects in the computer labs. This includes approving student blogs, linking to the central access site, and troubleshooting a variety of technical and content issues related to publishing.

7. Manage student posts and comments for content. It is helpful to select a blogging platform that allows you to approve student comments before they are published. It is also helpful to establish guidelines for acceptable content and grammar for comments.

Beyond the Basics

The blogging journey continued. Paulson felt the need to offer extensions to the unit as a way to foster more critical thinking. The extensions involved students comparing and contrasting events, analyzing character actions, and synthesizing quotes. She also posted questions involving elements of literature, for example: "Which quote in Chapter 8 is an example of foreshadowing?" Student responses were insightful, connected to culture, and were proof of a deepened understanding of text. In another post, she asked students to analyze the meaning of a well-known saying, and then give an example of their own. One student gave her response in Spanish, "No hagas lo que no quieres que te hagan." (English translation: Don't do what you don't want others to do to you—a powerful quote.)

Throughout the novel study, Paulson kept student blogging purposeful and tried to connect the big ideas in the ELA standards to student prompts. For example, one of the big ideas is theme, so she posted a question that dealt specifically with one of the book's themes:

> At one point in the story, the protagonist is in the mountains and a jar is dropped from a helicopter with a note inside. The note reads "Stay where you are. We are here to help you." Predict what the protagonist will do.

The question connects to the theme of trust: How do you know who to trust when you are in a desperate situation? With each blogging opportunity, students became more comfortable with the process and the depth in their responses increased, including length, use of text evidence, and an increased number of student responses to one another. Blogging is engaging, motivating, and allows for the use of a new skill set.

Reflections on the Project

From a teacher's perspective, Paulson felt that student voice was heard as evidenced in comparing activities done before the class started blogging and activities during and after the blogging. The preblogging activity began with students doing a *quick write* in response to the prompt, "I think those who are undocumented should/should not cross the border because ___." (Students needed to choose between different responses and then give an explanation.) Even though students were asked after responding to do a *turn and talk* with their partners, because of time constraints only a few students shared their thoughts with the large group. However, after students had the opportunity to blog, not only could they read everyone's response, but they could also ask clarifying questions. A clarifying question can support a student in thinking deeply about his or her response to a posed question.

It is important for students to understand that because of our different experiences, we have different perspectives and much is gained by sharing them. It's all part of the importance of student voice and fostering a community of learners. With this activity, the playing field was leveled and all students participated due to the nonthreatening environment established by blogging.

Not only did the students use technology for communication, they also used it to think harder about text. Research, such as that illustrated by Keene and Zimmerman in *Mosaic of Thought* (Heinemann, 2007), supports the notion of the importance of student response in deepening the understanding of text. Additionally, the teacher was able to respond to each student's blog with either a comment or a question to further their thinking, asking them to use evidence from the text to support their answer or possibly pointing out the correct use of a particular term or skill. Students looked forward to blogging and excitedly anticipated their classmates' comments: in a way, this was similar to receiving a letter from a pen pal, but without the "snail mail" response time.

The results of a post-blog activity survey we conducted includes these comments from three different students:

> "The one thing blogging helped me to do better was to tell how I felt about the story in a new and different format."

> "The one thing blogging helped me to do better was answering questions and writing them in our blog. I thought it was helpful because then I better understood the story."

> "One thing blogging helped me to do was to understand other students and listen to their comments."

Something to keep in mind is that once students have a blog account, they can continue to use it throughout the year. Blogging can be done in other subjects as well. Certainly, we are looking forward to blogging next year!

Assessment and Standards Addressed

Assessment

The accountability facet of the project was done through a rubric. Students were assessed on the following:

- Quality of writing

- Presentation

- Language arts content

- Community

Students had just finished an "Elements of Literature" unit and Paulson wanted students to use a common vocabulary when discussing novels. For community, students got points for how many comments they made on one another's blog.

Standards

ISTE Standards for Students (ISTE Standards•S)

The standard most strongly addressed in this project is Communication and Collaboration.

2.   Communication and Collaboration

Students use digital media and environments to communicate and work collaboratively, including at a distance, to support individual learning and contribute to the learning of others.

The use of *Crossing the Wire* for our novel study unit clearly addresses indicator 2c:

   c.   develop cultural understanding and global awareness by engaging with learners of other cultures

Common Core State Standards for ELA

Although our district aligns units of instruction with state standards, some districts now use the Common Core State Standards. Our Minnesota state standards and Common Core ELA standards parallel each other, "Reading: Literature—Key Ideas and Detail" being the Common Core equivalent for this unit.

Key Ideas and Details: CCSS.ELA-Literacy

CCRA.R.1   Read closely to determine what the text says explicitly and to make logical inferences from it; cite specific textual evidence when writing or speaking to support conclusions drawn from the text.

CCRA.R.2   Determine central ideas or themes of a text and analyze their development; summarize the key supporting details and ideas.

CCRA.R.3   Analyze how and why individuals, events, or ideas develop and interact over the course of a text.
(www.corestandards.org/ELA-Literacy/CCRA/R)

The specific English language arts standards we intended to address in our book study include the following:

- describing how a particular story or drama plot unfolds in a series of episodes that include character change

- citing textual evidence to support analysis of text as well as inferencing

- determining theme through particular details

- determining theme and how it is supported through details

SECTION III

story writing

CHAPTER 8

Graphic Novel–Style Writing Projects
>   Grades 6–12 / Ages 11–18 / Middle and High School
>   Microsoft Word or Apache OpenOffice word processor

CHAPTER 9

Interactive Fiction
>   Grades 6–12 / Ages 11–18 / Middle and High School
>   Interactive fiction (IF) software

CHAPTER 10

Language Learning between the Panels:
Comics, Performance, Shakespeare, and ELL
>   Grade 7 / Ages 12–13 / Middle School
>   Pixton or other online comics creator

CHAPTER 8

Graphic Novel–Style Writing Projects

Mark Gura

LEVEL

Grades 6–12 / Ages 11–18 / Middle and High School

TECHNOLOGY

Microsoft Word or Apache OpenOffice
word processing

LITERACY

Story writing, report writing, illustrating

STANDARDS

ISTE Standards•S, Common Core ELA (Writing, *W*)

Creating original projects in the style of graphic novels proved to be one of the most popular activities in my middle school fine arts classes. Not only did the students love it, but it was an activity that piqued the interest of co-teachers who were involved in teaching core curriculum subjects. They could see that the practice had a strong literacy learning potential. Further, while I was focused on having students learn the techniques and nuances of graphic novels and instilling an appreciation for this art, I left the choice of subject up to the students. As a result, students often brought content from science, social studies, and ELA classes into their graphic novel projects.

This activity was effective and practical for a number of reasons. First, the graphic novel is a literary form that most of my students were familiar with and had high interest in. Second, drawing comics was an activity many students enjoyed greatly; in fact, it bordered on an obsession for a good number of them. There were several students in each of my classes who were adept at the approach and were more than capable of assisting classmates.

Why Graphic Novels?

One unique aspect of graphic novels is that the author is not tied to traditional linear storytelling, as would be the case in a traditional novel or short story, or even in a traditional comic strip. Using attention-directing devices like arrows, readers are often invited to leapfrog about the page following a free-form approach to sequence.

The high level of engagement created by the visual art aspect of the project provides momentum that in turn engages students in the writing dimension of the project. While extended text passages are not unheard of in graphic novels, communication that must be accomplished in text is generally done with only a few sentences at a time. All text must be subordinated to the overall design of the page, and this calls on students to make economy in their writing a priority. Sequencing of events and story elements is another dimension of storytelling that is critical in this genre.

Before attempting to teach graphic novel creation, I recommend that the teacher read several different graphic novels to become familiar with the genre and its conventions. Comic strips are generally short and linear in sequence and layout, with panels of roughly equal size. Comic books push the envelope further; longer in length, telling a full story, and sometimes with devices to break strict sequence format. Graphic novels are often more freeform with odd-shaped panels of clearly different sizes and orientations. They can use a variety of devices to indicate where the reader's attention should go. As they are more serious undertakings, the text and images work hard to convey plot and story details, important concepts and facts, as well as mood and the emotional dimension of a good story. And of course, there are many instances of the line between comic strip, comic book, and graphic novel being blurry or the envelope being pushed in one direction or another.

Tools and Techniques

Technology can make original student graphic novel–style projects easy to do and highly successful. The emergence of online comic creation resources over the past few years has brought the act of creating comic strips within the grasp of the average person who isn't artistically talented. These are remarkable resources and are popular for good reason. I recommend you check them out.

These are a few free online comic creation resources often used by teachers:

Strip Generator: http://stripgenerator.com

Write Comics: http://writecomics.com

Comic Creator: www.readwritethink.org/files/resources/interactives/comic

These two sites offer more sophisticated resources, which are more challenging to use and are not necessarily free:

Pixton: www.pixton.com

Chogger: www.chogger.com

There's another resource to consider: Current versions of Microsoft Word or Apache OpenOffice can produce wonderful, graphically rich pages that are composed of a blend of images and text. While the images are generally not produced directly in these applications, the programs are a nimble vehicle into which images are easily inserted and then processed. Images can either be drawn directly by students and then scanned and saved in a graphic file format or searched for and downloaded from copyright-safe sources on the web.

There are several advantages to using digital images to create graphic novel pages over the laborious process of drawing by hand. Chief among these is the ability to size, move, and position images, as well as the fact that an image can be used as many times as needed. For non-art teachers there is a great advantage, too, in creating these works on a computer screen: There is no need for special materials, facilities, or classroom management consideration.

Beyond the marriage of writing to visual art, the graphic novel format involves another facet of design—the design of text and typography. Technology not only makes this possible but engrossing and pleasurable as well. Word processing programs provide a vast palette of options in font, symbols, style, and color, all of which can help students to focus on text and its communicative function.

Microsoft Word

Microsoft (MS) Word is very well suited to producing graphic novel projects. It provides numerous functions that are essential to the genre and its form.

The ability to insert objects. Graphics such as photos; scanned student drawings; downloaded, appropriated images; chart-style infographics saved in JPG or other graphics file format; and text boxes can be inserted into an MS Word document.

The ability to manipulate objects. Graphics inserted into an MS Word document can be sized, positioned, and tilted or rotated at will. Choosing the "Tight" Text Wrap option makes moving and positioning the object easy.

The ability to add borders. Objects like graphics or text boxes can be given a border for which there are a great many possible variations. This adds to the graphic novel look of the page elements.

There is a large palette of shapes. Shapes such as arrows, lines, and stars can be inserted, sized, and moved about, also adding to the classic graphic novel look of a page. They may also be used to help the writer direct the reader's attention from one element to another.

The ability to manipulate text. Text can be inserted into a text box or shape which can be sized, positioned, and tilted or rotated. Text inserted within these items (text boxes and objects) may be adjusted for size, font, style, color, and so forth.

The ability to move callouts. Callouts are dialogue balloons and thought bubbles (which are essential devices for comics and graphic novels). Like other objects, callouts may be inserted, moved, and adjusted at will.

A Wide Variety of Applications

Within the realm of storytelling, graphic novels provide a great platform to support students in developing a variety of writing skills. These include developing characters and story settings, as well as dialogue and plot. Assignments that lend themselves well to using the graphic novel format are writing original stories, creating procedural narratives, and communicating what they've learned about something—a current events story, for instance. Or, students might use the graphic novel format to demonstrate comprehension of a book—an alternative type of book report.

One project my students enjoyed that had strong impact involved using the graphic novel format as an alternative variety of research report. The assignment was for students to pick a scientist whose work was significant from both the scientific perspective and from a historical or social perspective; in other words, a scientific breakthrough that had a strong effect on the lives of people. My instructions included having the scientists introduce themselves and then explain the background of their breakthroughs: why they did what they did, how they did it, and what the results were. Albert Einstein (Figure 8.1), Marie Curie, and Jane Goodall were among the scientists chosen by students for these reports.

This sort of project-based literacy actualizes a good many ideals of literacy instruction: authentic writing projects, storytelling, character development, writing informational text, and student publishing. The special bonus this particular approach offers is that it is interdisciplinary, addressing required learning in core curriculum subjects, and modeling for students how essential skills carry across subject areas.

Figure 8.1 Graphic novel format used as an alternative research report

A Unique Platform for Improving Writing Skills

The format of the graphic novel approach to content creation offers a number of unique slants on literacy learning. For one thing, it offers an opportunity for students to learn from grappling with spoken dialogue and text representations of a character's thoughts. While deciding what part of the story can be accomplished visually or through written text, or as a hybrid of both, students must focus on how to convey the gist of a story or nonfiction functional text both economically and effectively. As the elements of a narrative are isolated graphically in a dialogue balloon or thought bubble, the small amount of text within them offers a perfect situation for reflection on grammar, voice, punctuation, and content—all perfectly contextualized.

While some descriptive writing can be replaced by the graphics, graphic novels frequently use short written passages placed in text boxes to convey background information about the story. The graphic novel approach also offers a way to visualize and understand the relative importance of elements to the whole piece, both of those things included and those left out. These are all part of the conventions of language specific to this genre.

Knowing that the finished product will have a polished, professional look and will be published for an authentic audience engages students very powerfully. How can you publish a word processed document that is a mixture of visual graphics and text? There are numerous approaches. For example, by saving the document as a PDF file and uploading it to a document sharing web-based resource like Scribd or Docstoc, publication is easy to accomplish.

Scribd: www.scribd.com

Docstoc: www.docstoc.com

Such resources now offer a variety of privacy and security options that help tremendously to eliminate risks associated with putting student work online. These sites can also be used as social networking resources that make the distribution of this content easy and effective.

Standards Addressed

While there are many possible points of alignment between this practice and the Common Core State Standards for ELA, there is a particularly clear connection in the Writing standards under the Text Types and Purposes section (especially W.5.3: Write narratives to develop real or imagined experiences or events using effective technique, descriptive details, and clear event sequences) and the Production and Distribution of Writing section (W.5.4–W.5.6).

Similarly, there are possible areas of alignment to most of the ISTE Standards•S, with particularly strong connections to the areas of Creativity and Innovation (especially 1b: Create original works as a means of personal or group expression) as well. Communication and Collaboration (especially 2b: Communicate information and ideas effectively to multiple audiences using a variety of media and formats.)

ISTE Standards for Students (ISTE Standards•S)

1. **Creativity and Innovation**

   Students demonstrate creative thinking, construct knowledge, and develop innovative products and processes using technology. Students:

   a. apply existing knowledge to generate new ideas, products, or processes

   b. create original works as a means of personal or group expression

2. **Communication and Collaboration**

   Students use digital media and environments to communicate and work collaboratively, including at a distance, to support individual learning and contribute to the learning of others. Students:

   a. interact, collaborate, and publish with peers, experts, or others employing a variety of digital environments and media

   b. communicate information and ideas effectively to multiple audiences using a variety of media and formats

3. **Research and Information Fluency**

   Students apply digital tools to gather, evaluate, and use information. Students:

   c. evaluate and select information sources and digital tools based on the appropriateness to specific tasks

4. **Critical Thinking, Problem Solving, and Decision Making**

   Students use critical-thinking skills to plan and conduct research, manage projects, solve problems, and make informed decisions using appropriate digital tools and resources. Students:

   d. use multiple processes and diverse perspectives to explore alternative solutions

6. **Technology Operations and Concepts**

   Students demonstrate a sound understanding of technology concepts, systems, and operations. Students:

   a. understand and use technology systems

   b. select and use applications effectively and productively

Common Core State Standards

Writing

Text Types and Purposes

W.5.2   Write informative/explanatory texts to examine a topic and convey ideas and information clearly.

- Introduce a topic clearly, provide a general observation and focus, and group related information logically; include formatting (e.g., headings), illustrations, and multimedia when useful to aiding comprehension.

- Develop the topic with facts, definitions, concrete details, quotations, or other information and examples related to the topic.

- Link ideas within and across categories of information using words, phrases, and clauses (e.g., in contrast, especially).

- Use precise language and domain-specific vocabulary to inform about or explain the topic.

- Provide a concluding statement or section related to the information or explanation presented.

W.5.3   Write narratives to develop real or imagined experiences or events using effective technique, descriptive details, and clear event sequences.

- Orient the reader by establishing a situation and introducing a narrator and/or characters; organize an event sequence that unfolds naturally.

- Use narrative techniques, such as dialogue, description, and pacing, to develop experiences and events or show the responses of characters to situations.

- Use a variety of transitional words, phrases, and clauses to manage the sequence of events.

- Use concrete words and phrases and sensory details to convey experiences and events precisely.

- Provide a conclusion that follows from the narrated experiences or events.

Production and Distribution of Writing

W.5.4   Produce clear and coherent writing in which the development and organization are appropriate to task, purpose, and audience.

W.5.5   With guidance and support from peers and adults, develop and strengthen writing as needed by planning, revising, editing, rewriting, or trying a new approach.

W.5.6   With some guidance and support from adults, use technology, including the internet, to produce and publish writing as well as to interact and collaborate with others; demonstrate sufficient command of keyboarding skills to type a minimum of two pages in a single sitting.

Conclusion

Graphic novel–style projects offer high interest and numerous opportunities for students to focus on and hone their writing skills. The simultaneous emergence of this new writing genre and the availability of tools needed to teach and engage students in creating graphic novels, along with today's need for updated, relevant activities, represent a powerful invitation to give this approach a try.

CHAPTER 9

Interactive Fiction

Gerald W. Aungst

LEVEL

Grades 6–12 / Ages 11–18 / Middle and High School

TECHNOLOGY

Interactive fiction (IF) software

LITERACY

Story reading, story writing

STANDARDS

ISTE Standards•S, Common Core ELA (Writing, *W*, and Reading: Literature, *RL*)

Tenth grade students straggle into their English class and pull out their copies of The Grapes of Wrath. *The teacher stands behind her lectern and opens her copy of the book. "Last night," she says, "we read Chapter 3. Can someone tell us your interpretation of the chapter?"*

After a few uncomfortable moments, and hearing nothing more than the shuffling of a few feet and one boy quietly clearing his throat at the back of the classroom, the teacher selects a student at random. The girl, Michele, is a tad startled. She hesitates at first, then briefly explains that she thinks the turtle in the chapter represents our struggle to get through life.

"No, I'm sorry, that's incorrect," pronounces the teacher.

Incorrect? Michele thinks. How can it be incorrect? She asked for my interpretation. That was my interpretation. Michele decides she isn't going to share her thoughts in this class any more.

This scene is based on a true story, and it highlights some of what students sometimes find difficult or frustrating about literacy studies. Instead of reading as a means of communication—a fascinating asynchronous interchange between the author's mind and the reader's—it becomes a dreary guessing game for many students: They must discover an inscrutable message that the author has hidden behind layers of obscure literary references and figurative language and which only the enlightened few will ever fully grasp.

IF = Excitement and Motivation for Reading and Writing

Interactive fiction (IF) is a tool that teachers can use to bring excitement and motivation to students who may not care for other kinds of reading. Simple and free resources exist that allow anyone to compose works of interactive fiction. With these tools, IF can also help students recognize the deep relationships between reader and writer, highlight the importance of writing with audience in mind, and demystify some of the mechanics of the writing process.

Developed originally as a form of computer gaming in the 1970s, interactive fiction grew in popularity through the 1980s. As better computer graphics brought about the explosion of video games, IF's popularity declined, but it remains a highly valuable teaching resource for both reading and writing instruction.

Interactive fiction stories are text-based computer programs in which a story is told in small segments. The player (reader), instead of passively receiving the text in a linear fashion as with standard forms of literature, must interact with the story as a participant, moving through the environment, manipulating objects, and conversing with other characters.

Interactive fiction can be a unique and engaging way for students to practice and apply literacy skills on several levels. When using IF in the classroom, consider developing student skills in two phases: first as a reader, playing existing games and learning the rules of the genre; then as a writer, creating original works of interactive fiction. Throughout this chapter, we will use the words "reader" and "player" interchangeably to refer to the person who is interacting with the story. Likewise, "author" and "writer" refer to the person who creates that story.

Several different software programs are involved in using interactive fiction in the classroom. One program, the interpreter, reads and interacts with the story—think of this as the IF version of an ebook reader. To create original IF stories, a separate program is used—this is like a specialized word processor. The story file itself is then like the ebook document you load into the ebook reader. The next section gives you more information about choosing and locating the software packages.

Learning with Interactive Fiction

Following is an example of a typical exchange between the player (reader) and the program. The player (reader) is prompted to interact by the ">" symbol, and the words **in bold** are the player's typed-in commands to the game.

Here, the player (reader) is shown the starting point for the game, Room 9 in the main character's school, and the main goal that needs to be accomplished: to turn in his missing assignment. This will prove to be a bit complicated as the game progresses, and the player (reader) will have to solve various puzzles to get the assignment finished and turned in. By telling the story what to do—"**get envelope**," "**give it to teacher**," and so forth—the player interacts with and changes the environment, and the story reacts to those changes by responding with dialogue and action.

Room 9

Your desk is surprisingly organized today, probably because you had nothing better to do during recess yesterday than to clean it out. On your desk are a clean sheet of paper and an origami fortuneteller, and inside it are a binder, a white envelope, a supply box, and a blue folder.

Mrs. McClintock is marking some papers, patiently waiting for you to turn in your missing assignment.

> **get envelope**
Taken.

> **give it to teacher**
You hand the note to Mrs. McClintock.

"Here, my mom sent this in."

"Thank you, Jamie," she replies.

Mrs. McClintock reads the note. "You need to go pick up your brother's homework folder from Mr. Bradley's room next door. Better do it now so that you don't forget."

> **go south**

Main Hallway

Sunshine pours through skylights along this broad, bright, clean hallway which continues east and west from here. Your homeroom is to the north and the school library is to the south.

One of the most interesting aspects of writing interactive fiction is the realization that the main character—enacted by the reader—might not do what the writer of the story expects. The writer must anticipate many different actions the player might make and prepare responses for them. For example, in the sequence above, the player (reader) could just as easily have decided to open the envelope and read the letter, play with the fortuneteller, talk to Mrs. McClintock, or try to leave the room without permission.

Resources Required

To use IF in your classroom, you will need computers and some free software. IF stories are available in several formats, and you will need an interpreter program to access them. The Inform 7 website (www.inform7.com) offers a good list of available programs on its "Playing Interactive Fiction" page. There are also interpreters for mobile devices.

Next you will need a source of literature. One of the most comprehensive is Baf's Guide to the IF Archive (http://wurb.com/if), which offers nearly three thousand different titles. Be aware, however, that every genre is represented within the scope of interactive fiction, including adult titles. It is best to hand pick a few appropriate titles that you will use in your instruction. Although there are places such as Parchment (www.iplayif.com) where IF can be played online without dedicated software, these sites are likely to be filtered.

For writing interactive fiction, there are several development systems. The two most popular are TADS (www.tads.org) and Inform 7 (www.inform7.com). TADS is very much like a computer programming language, while Inform is designed to work with a more natural language interface, making it a more likely choice for school implementation.

Baf's Guide to the IF Archive: http://wurb.com/if

Inform 7 Download: http://inform7.com/download

Inform 7 Interpreter Program: www.inform7.com/if/interpreters/

Parchment: www.iplayif.com

TADS: www.tads.org

Implementation

Though many people play IF recreationally as an individual pursuit, in the classroom interactive fiction is best used as a collaborative learning activity, both for reading ("playing") and writing. Have students work together with a partner to play their first game of IF. Good choices for this first experience are *The Dreamhold* by Andrew Plotkin; *Bronze,* by Emily Short (choose the edited, PG version); and *Mrs. Pepper's Nasty Secret,* by Jim Aikin and Eric Eve. These games include built-in tutorials that help first-time users navigate the idiosyncratic grammar of IF commands.

The Dreamhold: http://eblong.com/zarf/zweb/dreamhold

Bronze: http://emshort.wordpress.com/my-work/

Mrs. Pepper's Nasty Secret: http://ifdb.tads.org/viewgame?id=dcvk7bgbqeb0a71s

Game transcripts, created by entering the command "**transcript**," are extremely helpful both to the teacher and to the students for later reference. The transcript is a complete record of the entire game, including all commands entered by the player. Like players studying a game film, students can review and analyze their work, reflect on their comprehension of the story, and learn the conventions of IF.

Playing IF brings to the surface many comprehension strategies. In order to interact successfully with the story, the player must understand the text. Also, the student's thought process is made visible through the specific actions he or she chooses. The game mechanics provide additional motivation to comprehend. The player also gets immediate feedback: If the reader does not comprehend the text, the attempted solutions will not work. The reader must also revisit prior text to solve problems, deepening and enriching the understanding of the text.

From Reader to Writer

To take the process to a deeper level, have students try their hand at writing their own interactive fiction. A good first taste of writing IF is simply to design a small room and describe it and its contents. This seemingly simple task—which would result in a short paragraph in a standard story—can become a lengthy project. IF conventions require that every object mentioned in a room description have its own description, so the player who examines it gets a reasonable response. Thus a small room will require paragraph upon paragraph of description.

Sharing a work in progress with another student can also lend insight into the relationship between writer and reader. Often when students are asked to peer review, they have difficulty expressing their thinking and their responses to the text. A transcript of a first-time reader's exploration can help make explicit the gap between the author's intention and the reader's interpretation.

Options for publishing student work are many. Beyond simply sharing game files with each other or posting them online to share publicly, there is an annual IF competition hosted by the Interactive Fiction Community (www.ifcomp.org) where anyone can enter a work and have it reviewed by the IF community. The Interactive Fiction Archive (www.ifarchive.org) also encourages contributions to be uploaded to their index.

Interactive Fiction Archive: www.ifarchive.org

Interactive Fiction Competition: www.ifcomp.org

Student Population

Interactive fiction is most appropriate for middle and high school students. While language arts is the most logical curriculum connection, IF can also be a tool for developing text-based simulations in science or social studies. The reasoning skill required to write effective IF makes it a good fit for mathematics or computer science courses as well.

Student Work Sample

Students developing an interactive fiction project using Inform 7 are creating not just a work of fiction, but also a computer program. Because it is a programming language, the Inform 7 text that a student writes is called "source code," and is a blend of the story text, natural language computer commands, and some project-specific ways to encode objects and actions.

The entire "story" is contained in an Inform 7 project file. The Inform 7 program helps the students organize all of the text files that comprise the project, and also contains an extensive help and tutorial system to support students who are learning how to write these game programs.

This is an example of what the source code looks like for an Inform 7 project, and is typical of what students might be able to generate after working with the program for a while:

Room 9 is a room. "[if visited] You notice a new flake of peeling paint to the left of the chalkboard that you hadn[']t seen before, but otherwise, every detail of your fourth grade classroom is unchanged from yesterday ... and the day before ... and the day before that ... [otherwise] You've spent what seems like thousands of endless, dreary, winter days in this room during what should have been your recess period. But of course the weather didn[']t cooperate.

In a more traditional piece of fiction, this might be a description that appears somewhere early in the story. In IF, however, the author must tell the program when and how to reveal the description to the reader. In this case, the game gives one description if the player has already visited the room, and a different one the first time the player sees it. Features like this give a great deal of creative freedom to student authors, allowing them to create a story that adapts itself to the changing situation in the game.

The writer can then go on to describe even the smallest details of a space, which permits the reader to explore at will:

The chalkboard is scenery in Room 9. The description of the chalkboard is "There is not much available space on the board for Mrs. McClintock to write–she has all sorts of notes and posters neatly taped to it for reference. In the little bit of chalkboard left, you see:[/l]February 23[/l] Schedule:[/l]9:00–Reading[/l]10:15–Gym[/l]10:45—Math[/l]11:45– Recess/Lunch[/l]12:45–Science[/l]1:30–Social Studies[/l]2:15–Writing Workshop[/l]3:00–DEAR Time". The chalkboard is familiar.

Dialogue and action can be programmed similarly, giving characters a broad variety of things to say and do depending on what the player says or does, and allowing many different paths through the story. Unlike standard forms of fiction, where there is one linear plot, the writer must imagine many possibilities and anticipate many different ways the main character can act.

Assessment and Standards Addressed

It is not recommended to formally assess student reading of interactive fiction. The nature of the medium creates a natural self-assessment since the game itself provides feedback about the player's success in comprehension and problem solving.

When students begin to write their own interactive fiction, a highly effective formative assessment is for student teams to play each other's games. The respective teams can then sit down together with the game transcripts and debrief the game play, discussing what is effective, what is confusing, and what isn't working as intended.

The following standards are addressed:

ISTE Standards for Students (ISTE Standards•S)

1. **Creativity and Innovation**
   b. create original works as a means of personal or group expression

2. **Communication and Collaboration**
   d. contribute to project teams to produce original works or solve problems

4. **Critical Thinking, Problem Solving, and Decision Making**
   a. identify and define authentic problems and significant questions for investigation
   b. plan and manage activities to develop a solution or complete a project

6. **Technology Operations and Concepts**
   c. troubleshoot systems and applications

Common Core State Standards for ELA

Reading: Literature

RL8.3   Analyze how particular lines of dialogue or incidents in a story or drama propel the action, reveal aspects of a character, or provoke a decision.

RL.11–12.4   Determine the meaning of words and phrases as they are used in the text, including figurative and connotative meanings; analyze the impact of specific word choices on meaning and tone, including words with multiple meanings or language that is particularly fresh, engaging, or beautiful.

Writing

W.11–12.3   Write narratives to develop real or imagined experiences or events using effective technique, well-chosen details, and well-structured event sequences.

W.11–12.6   Use technology, including the internet, to produce, publish, and update individual or shared writing products in response to ongoing feedback, including new arguments or information.

W.11–12.10.   Write routinely over extended time frames (time for research, reflection, and revision) and shorter time frames (a single sitting or a day or two) for a range of tasks, purposes.

Further Reading

Desilets, B. (n.d.). *Teaching and learning with interactive fiction.* Retrieved from http://bdesilets.com/if/

English, D. (2008, July). MHS (Montgomery Township High School, NJ) Interactive Fiction Workshop. [Agenda]. Retrieved from https://sites.google.com/site/dgenglish7/home

Inform 7. (n.d.). *Teach with Inform.* Retrieved from http://inform7.com/teach/

McCall, J. (2005, 2006, 2007). Inform simulation assignments and rubrics. Retrieved from http://gamingthepast.net/simulation-design/inform-7/inform-simulation-assignments-and-rubrics/

Short, E. (n.d.) *Teaching IF.* Retrieved from http://emshort.wordpress.com/how-to-play/teaching-if/

CHAPTER 10

Language Learning between the Panels
Comics, Performance, Shakespeare, and ELL

Christopher Shamburg

LEVEL

Grade 7 / Ages 12–13 / Middle School

TECHNOLOGY

Pixton or other online comics creator

LITERACY

Reading, writing, performing

STANDARDS

ISTE Standards•S, Common Core (Reading: Literature, *RL*; Writing, *W*; Speaking and Listening, *SL*; and Language, *L*)

A lot can happen in the blink of an eye. Even more can happen when that blink takes a minute, an hour, or a day. This is the power of the gutter in comics. The gutter is the space between the individual panels in a comic. It is the place where two individual images synthesize to become one idea. It is a place where the reader intuitively uses inference and imagination to make meaning. In *Understanding Comics,* Scott McCloud describes the gutter as "host to much of the magic and mystery that are at the very heart of comics" (1994, p. 66).

This quiet space between the panels can also be a powerful place for learning language.

A Tale of Two Comics

Look at the two strips in Figure 10.1 and notice how the gutter works between the images to create different stories.

Figure 10.1 Two stories; two gutter examples

This chapter presents a lesson on the use of the gutter, using the gutter as a prompt for students' creativity, inference, and communication skills. It employs free, user-friendly Web 2.0 resources. Students are given a starting image and an ending image, and they must create the action that connects them. This approach engages students in the traditional literacies of reading, writing, and speaking as well as new literacies associated with multiple mediums, remix, and appropriation (Jenkins, 2007; Lankshear & Knobel, 2011; Shamburg, 2008).

The performance in this activity is also an extremely beneficial component. The performance helps with authentic language development and is also an excellent way to develop students' executive function. Executive function is a collection of cognitive skills related to higher-order thinking which has gained the attention of neuroscientists, cognitive psychologists, and educators. Executive function has a correlation to success in school and in life that is higher than IQ and, unlike traditional notions of IQ, is completely "growable" (Diamond, 2009). Key components of executive function are working memory, impulse control, flexible thinking, and mind/body integration. These are all activities involved in performance. This particular activity is an excellent prompt to get students to move purposefully and coordinate words, gestures, and actions.

There's a wide variety of grades and students for whom this work is appropriate and effective. You can choose the sophistication of the images, the "space" of the gutter, and the expectations for students to fill it. For example, in a second grade class, you may have an initial image of a birthday party with smiling children and then a second image of an unhappy child. You can prompt the students to create a story about what happened in between.

Technology

All of the examples here were created with Pixton, an online comic creator. Other comic creation tools are Plasq's Comic Life or Make Beliefs Comix.

Make Beliefs Comix: www.makebeliefscomix.com

Plasq's Comic Life: http://plasq.com/products/comiclife

Pixton: www.pixton.com

These programs simplify the more technical aspects of comic creation and let a user focus on the creative aspects of production. These programs allow you to save, edit, revise, and share your work.

If you do not have access to these tools, simply importing, organizing, and printing images in a word processing program can work well too. The activity described here was done in a classroom with a limited amount of technology. If you have more technology, such as a laptop cart or lab with five or six computer stations, students can have more input on the actual comic creation.

Though the content and objectives were different in each case, there are three common elements to this activity:

1. a starting image

2. an ending image

3. the students' goal of connecting those images through writing, speaking, and performance

Shakespeare, Comics, and Performance

These connections of action and language are especially strong in Shakespeare. Performance-based approaches based on the premise that Shakespeare's plays were meant to be enacted and not simply read have been popular for the last 25 years (Young, 2009). This fact, along with the increased emphasis on authentic assessment and multiple intelligences, has made performance-based approaches a growing trend in the teaching of Shakespeare (Lomonico, 2009). An excellent resource for getting started with performance-based approaches is *Shakespeare Set Free* (O'Brien, 1992) and the Folger Shakespeare Library's Division of Education (www.folger.edu/education).

One fact that has engaged eager performers and overzealous editors is that Shakespeare wrote very little stage direction. Most of the staging of a play or movie is based on implicit stage directions. This gives students the opportunity to understand that language is open to interpretation and that nonverbal communication—tone, gestures, movement, and facial expressions—can change the meaning of words.

Below is dialogue from a pivotal scene in *Othello* between Iago and Othello. In this scene Iago is trying to sow the seeds of jealousy in Othello. Othello believes that Iago is his loyal friend, but Iago is actually trying to provoke jealousy by hinting about Othello's wife's infidelity. Shakespeare gives us no stage direction during this scene and lets the performers and readers fill in the blanks.

> *Othello:*   By heaven I'll know thy thoughts Iago.
>
> *Iago:*   You cannot if my heart were in your hands.
>   Nor shall not, whilst it is in my custody.

Is Othello angered or saddened by Iago's suggestions? Does he react violently (a foreshadowing of his later rage)? Or desperately (an indication of his sorrow for the loss of his true love)? Students get to explore both of these complex and important interpretations through the simple use of images. In activities like this, production is analysis.

The goals of this activity will be for students to

- synthesize language, vocal techniques, and physical gestures to convey meaning;

- draw inferences and conclusions based on context;

- analyze character, plot, and other literary devices; and

- explore the relationship between characters.

Working in groups of two, students are given a starting image and an ending image (Figure 10.2). They must perform the lines above to get them from start to ending. Put another way, the two students will pose like the characters in the first panel. Speaking the lines, they will move from the initial poses to the poses in the second, ending panel. The meaning they find in the lines should be conveyed by the performance.

Figure 10.2 Othello in the Gutter: two different takes

Extensions

This approach can work with any play and almost any scene in Shakespeare. I'd recommend beginning with two-person scenes and then moving to three- and four-person scenes. Here are some scenes and methods to vary the images in the comic panels:

- *Romeo and Juliet:* Does Romeo kill Tybalt by accident or on purpose?

- *Hamlet:* When Hamlet sees the ghost of his father, is he frightened, excited, or sad?

- *Macbeth:* Is there really a ghost of Banquo that Macbeth sees, or is it just his imagination?

ELL and Special Needs

Fault-tolerant activities such as the Shakespeare activity are well suited to English language learner classes. If students do the simple, basic activities, they will be successful. With this activity, success and learning can come easily to students with special needs as well as students who learn quickly in traditional ways.

Some students will put more in the gutter, but all should be able to create there. This activity lets all kids get creative, move with meaning, and take ownership of language.

Assessment and Standards Addressed

Assessment

During a performance assessment I find it useful to simply have a checklist with the various categories and observe the students performance. Table 10.1 gives a suggested way to weigh the different elements and goals:

Table 10.1 An Assessment Checklist

Elements and Goals	Percentage
Students used language, vocal techniques and physical activity to convey meaning.	25%
Students' nonverbal communication (gestures, tone, and expression) matched the context of the images.	25%
Students performed characters and spoke lines in an emotionally consistent way.	25%
Students began and ended in the designated poses.	25%

Standards Addressed

ISTE Standards for Students (ISTE Standards•S)

The Shakespeare activity addresses the following ISTE Standards•S.

1. **Creativity and Innovation**
   a. apply existing knowledge to generate new ideas, products, or processes
   b. create original works as a means of personal or group expression

2. **Communication and Collaboration**

    a. interact, collaborate, and publish with peers, experts, or others employing a variety of digital environments and media

    b. communicate information and ideas effectively to multiple audiences using a variety of media and formats

    d. contribute to project teams to produce original works or solve problems

4. **Critical Thinking, Problem Solving, and Decision Making**

    b. plan and manage activities to develop a solution or complete a project

    d. Use multiple processes and diverse perspectives to explore alternative solutions

Common Core State Standards for ELA

The gutter activity can be used in a variety of grades. If a gutter activity is done in a seventh grade classroom, here are the likely Common Core State Standards that would be met.

Reading: Literature

RL7.3   Analyze how particular elements of a story or drama interact (e.g., how setting shapes the characters or plot).

Writing

W.7.3   Write narratives to develop real or imagined experiences or events using effective technique, well-chosen details, and well-structured event sequences.

Speaking and Listening

SL.7.1   Engage effectively in a range of collaborative discussions (one-on-one, in groups, and teacher-led) with diverse partners on Grade 7 topics, texts, and issues, building on others' ideas and expressing their own clearly.

SL.7.2   Analyze the main ideas and supporting details presented in diverse media and formats (e.g., visually, quantitatively, orally) and explain how the ideas clarify a topic, text, or issue under study.

Language

L.7.1   Demonstrate command of the conventions of standard English grammar and usage when writing or speaking.

L.7.6   Acquire and use accurately grade-appropriate general academic and domain-specific words and phrases; gather vocabulary knowledge when considering a word or phrase important to comprehension or expression.

Conclusion

Capitalizing on the gutter is just one of the many ways comics can be used effectively in education. This approach gets students to collaborate in meaning-making by exploring the space between the images in comics. In between ELL and Shakespeare there are a variety of other applications for the connotative power of comics. Whether you are teaching figurative language, foreshadowing, vocabulary, making predictions, or understanding context clues, the gutter can be a helpful place. Incorporating with performance can exponentially improve language skills and the overall development of students.

Please feel free to download and remix any of the examples used in this chapter (www.pixton.com/cs272). You are also invited to email me with any questions—cshamburg@gmail.com.

References

Diamond, A. (2009). Learning, doing, being: A new science of education. Interviewed for On Being (podcast). Retrieved from www.onbeing.org/program/learning-doing-being-new-science-education/121

Jenkins, H. (2007). Confronting the challenges of participatory culture: Media education for the 21st century. Retrieved from http://digitallearning.macfound.org/atf/cf/%7B7E45C7E0-A3E0-4B89-AC9C-E807E1B0AE4E%7D/JENKINS_WHITE_PAPER.PDF

Lankshear, C., & Knobel, M. (2011). *New literacies* (3rd ed.). London, UK: Open University Press.

Lomonico, M. (2009). Shakespeare ruminations and innovations. *English Journal, 99*(1), pp. 21–28.

McCloud, S. (1994). *Understanding comics.* New York, NY: William Morrow.

O'Brien, P (1992). *Shakespeare set free.* New York, NY: Washington Square Press.

Shamburg, C. (2008). *NETS Curriculum Series: English language arts units for grades 9–12.* Eugene, OR: International Society for Technology in Education.

Young, R. (2009) … Is prologue. *English Journal, 99*(1), pp. 31–32.

SECTION IV

PERSUASIVE AND
argumentative
WRITING

CHAPTER 11

Building Literacy Radiolab-Style: Podcasting to Foster Speech and Debate Skills
    Grades 6–8 / Ages 11–14 / Middle School
    Radiolab podcast archive, Audacity, Sound Jay, Naturesongs

CHAPTER 12

Crafting an Argumentative Essay with Evernote
    Grades 6–12 / Ages 11–18 / Middle and High School
    Evernote

CHAPTER 13

Enhancing the Argument:
Using Threaded Discussion as a Persuasive Prewriting Tool
    Grade 8 / Ages 13–14 / Middle School
    Edublogs

CHAPTER 14

Building Literacy with Popular Web 2.0 Tools
    Grades K–12 / Ages 5–18 / Elementary, Middle, and High School
    Blogging, Edmodo, Wordle, Audacity

Building Literacy Radiolab-Style
Podcasting to Foster Speech and Debate Skills

Michele L. Haiken

LEVEL

Grades 6–8 / Ages 11–14 / Middle School

TECHNOLOGIES

Radiolab podcast archive, Audacity, Sound Jay, Naturesongs.com

LITERACY

Speech and debate, informative writing, persuasive writing

STANDARDS

ISTE Standards•S, Common Core ELA (Anchor Standards)

Looking for a new way to teach informative writing and public speaking, I was inspired by one of my favorite shows on National Public Radio. Radiolab hosts Jad Abumrad and Robert Krulwich combine reporting and documentary in fast-moving discussions about topics ranging from science and philosophy to human experience. Most of the topics are science related, but even I—an English teacher—am interested and engaged because of the way the hosts present the material.

The more I listened to various Radiolab podcasts, the more I realized each episode was actually a speech to inform about a specific scientific inquiry. The sound bites, music, and engaging discussions made me want to listen. I asked myself, "Why not have students create their own Radiolab-style podcasts about topics that are of interest to them?" I decided that we could post their podcasts on the school's website to share them with the school community and reach out to a wider audience.

Background of Practice

At my school, Speech and Debate is an academic elective for seventh and eighth grade students. The course is designed to cover the elements of informative and persuasive speech and writing. Speech and Debate might also be taught in the upper elementary grades as well as high school; teachers would need to modify these assignments depending on their students' skills and abilities. In fact, this assignment can be adapted for any secondary content area classroom. For Grades 9–12, modifications can be made to the podcasting topics, and different Radiolab examples can be shared with students at the beginning of the unit.

In my middle school, Speech and Debate class students spend the first ten weeks of the semester focusing on vocal expression and informative and persuasive speaking; the last ten weeks of the semester cover the elements of debate.

An informative speech is the first speech students write and present to the class. I wanted to have my students write a speech that involved real-world writing and addressed topics that were of interest to them. (I needed a change from the "Invent Your Own Candy" and "Great Vacation Travel Agency School" speeches students had written in the past!) I had recorded student speeches and debates in previous classes, but those were for students to listen to in order to glean tips on speaking. With the Radiolab-style podcasts, students knew that they were writing and speaking for recording purposes, with the ultimate goal of sharing their recordings with an online audience.

The objective with the Radiolab assignment was for students to create a podcast that was informative and intellectually stimulating. The unit took four weeks from the introduction of informative speaking, to studying the craft of a Radiolab podcast, to conducting research and writing scripts, and finally to the presentation of projects. Students met every day for this project and all the work was done in the classroom.

Setting Things Up

Radiolab can be seen as nonfiction text that extends across genres; as such, it was used as a model for students' writing and public speaking projects.

Hardware and Setup Resources

Here are the suggested hardware and setup resources for creating a Radiolab-style podcast:

Equipment

Computer (Mac or PC): desktop or laptop

Microphone: to record podcasts

Resources

Audacity: http://audacity.sourceforge.net
Free software program for recording and editing

Sound Jay: www.soundjay.com
Free sound effects to download

Naturesongs.com: www.naturesongs.com
Lots of free nature sounds

Radiolab Archives: www.radiolab.org/archive
Radiolab archive of podcast episodes

First Two Days

First, in the computer lab, students listened to two different Radiolab podcasts, and each student completed a graphic organizer/analysis worksheet to help direct their listening. Students worked independently and used headphones to listen to the podcasts individually. All work was done during class time. A teacher could adapt this part of the project by assigning the listening and reaction piece for homework or as a whole-class listening task.

During the first two days of the unit, students were to listen to one of two podcasts I had selected and complete an analysis worksheet (Figure 11.1). Next, they listened to a podcast of their own choice from the archives available on the Radiolab website.

Podcast Choice: _Numbers_

| Speech to Inform
How is this a speech to inform? What elements of informing do they bring to the radio show? | Public Speaking Style
What do you notice about Jad and Robert's speaking style and presentation? Articulation, rate, volume, pace, pause, distractions? | Other Observations & Noticings
Things that you would or would not want to model in your own radio lab podcast? |
|---|---|---|
| • They reference situations that are almost dependant on numbers
• A Johnny Cash Song about How he only has minutes to live
• They show how Mathematics and numbers influence an number of events in an average day | • Both very casual with their tones
• Add small jokes and reference things they know about each other
• Pause then bring-up new topics
• Very calm and don't talk loud but laugh pretty loud
• Always allow the other enough time to talk and don't cut them off | • Sound effects were simple
• A Song was used
• Foreshadowing
• Showing they are human and flawed
• A chill attitude
• Reference some off topic material but very little |

Figure 11.1 Student Radiolab analysis worksheet

Analyzing and Preparing

After listening, students discussed their observations and dissected the organizational structure of the podcast. In small groups, they responded to these questions:

1. In what way is this a speech to inform?

2. How effectively did the speech opening capture and hold your attention?

3. How did the speakers encourage the audience to learn?

4. What did the speakers do effectively to convey new information to the audience?

5. What were the speakers' strongest assets in informing the audience?

Introducing the Assignment

After analysis on the style and craft of the Radiolab podcasts, students were introduced to the assignment (Figure 11.2).

Many students selected topics from the suggested list—in particular, the question about whether we are alone in the universe. Other students came up with their own topics (for example: "Who is a stronger superhero, Batman or Superman?"). I gave each pair of students an outline to help them begin drafting their podcast manuscript (Form 11.1). Students followed the writing process of editing and revising using pen and paper or keyboarding their outline on the computer.

Students spent the first two days in the computer lab doing research and gathering support material to answer questions and learn more about their topics. Students gathered relevant information from multiple digital sources and integrated it into their podcasts. The elements of an informative speech were already discussed in earlier lessons. The outline reinforced the layout and style their podcasts should follow.

It was important to remind students that their speeches would be heard and not read, so students needed to understand the difference between writing an informative essay and crafting an informative podcast. We took a break during the drafting stage to examine the "moves" the Radiolab hosts made to keep listeners engaged and informed.

Students returned to their original graphic organizer/analysis worksheet for words or phrases that caught their attention during the podcast. I also catalogued and shared a handout with some of the phrases that caught my attention while listening to a variety of Radiolab podcasts (Form 11.2). Students were then able to model the transitions made by the Radiolab hosts and insert them into their own podcast manuscripts.

NPR's Radiolab is Looking for New Hosts!

You and your partner (yes, this speech to inform will be a tag-team presentation) need to prepare a demo podcast to be considered for the position.

Your demo speech/podcast should be about 3 to 4 minutes in length.

Remember, the idea behind Radiolab is that your ears are a portal to another world "Where sound illuminates ideas, and the boundaries blur between science, philosophy, and human experience. Big questions are investigated, tinkered with, and encouraged to grow. Bring your curiosity, and we'll feed it with possibility." (www.radiolab.org/about)

Thus, your topic to inform should concentrate on the questions surrounding science, philosophy, and/or human experience.

For those of you who are struggling with finding ideas, here are eight of the most popular "big questions" when it comes to humans and the universe in which we live:

How and why did the universe begin?
Is time travel physically or logically possible?
What's the point of living? Why are we here?
Could a computer have a mind?
What is death and should we fear it?
Are we alone in the universe?
How do we decide between right and wrong?

• • • • • • • •

This speech is an informative presentation. Your goal is to inform and teach your audience about your topic. First and foremost, select a topic that is interesting to you. It helps if you are knowledgeable on your topic; however, you can become knowledgeable on any topic through research. You also want to select a topic that will be intellectually stimulating to your audience. Always consider your audience, every step of the way.

Figure 11.2 Radiolab "Speech to Inform" assignment/invitation

Speech to Inform Outline
Radiolab-Style Format

Introduction

I.   (Attention Getter and Hook—Pull the audience in with something interesting)

II. (Reveal your topic—A glimpse at what you will be talking about)

III. (Preview Topic—Tell audience what you will cover during the speech)

IV. (Thesis Statement—One clear sentence that sums up what we will learn or discover during the speech to inform)

Body

I.   (First Main Point—A complete sentence)

    A.   (Sub Point—supports the main point) _____

        1. _____

            a. _____

            b. _____

    B.   (Sub Point—supports the main point) _____

        1. _____

            a. _____

            b. _____

    C.   (Sub Point—supports the main point) _____

        1. _____

            a. _____

            b. _____

    (Summary of Sub Points—Transition) _____

Conclusion

I.   (Summary of Main Points) _____

_____

II. (Memorable Close/Clincher—Tie this back to the Intro) _____

_____

Form 11.1 Radiolab-style podcast outline handout

Crafting a Radiolab-Style Podcast

What are some of the moves that Jad and Robert make during the podcast to help inform the audience?

_____

How can we make our Radiolab-style podcasts more informative?

_____

Here are some of the things Jad or Robert say that help the audience understand more deeply:

"Let's start with this …"

"I've got a story to tell. It's a good one. Imagine."
(Their first words in the Podcast "Lucy," 2/19/2010.)

Another hook to start the podcast.

"Here's why we included this story …"

This is where they begin to explain what the story was about and how it related to the main idea/topic of the podcast. They are making inferences and synthesizing what they have learned so far.

"So, what were you thinking …"

"What does she mean by this?"

Again, they are beginning to make sense of the "big quotes" and what the scientists are saying so that everyone can understand even if most of us don't have a PhD.

"In any case," *(retell what happened)*

"Maybe the strangest thing …"

"It appears …"

"So, what you are telling me …" *(synthesis and inferring—making sense of what is being said)*

"So, to set things up …"

"We have been listening to a really sad story …"

"The question we want to ask now …" *(After a big idea, refocus, redirect and connect back to main idea)*

"What should we all draw from this?" *(Setting up the closing or conclusion)*

*Also note there is usually some music in between the big ideas. After a big quote, Jad or Robert retell in their own words what the quote means and how it relates to music playing quietly in the background.

Form 11.2 The craft of Radiolab handout

Writing, Recording, and Editing

Students drafted their podcasts with their Radiolab podcast partners in the computer lab. Students worked side-by-side with their partners when compiling research and shared computers when they were producing their podcast manuscripts. This allowed me to circulate and offer individual support. I read over student podcast manuscripts, made edits, and asked questions in order to help students clarify wording. This time was also used to help students find sound effects (we used Sound Jay) to add to their podcasts that would help convey meaning and offer additional engagement for the listener.

Students had a day to practice the conversational style of speaking they heard on the original Radiolab podcasts. On the day of the recording, our school technology specialist helped record the podcasts. While we were recording each group's podcast, other groups were rehearsing and compiling sound effects.

Many of the podcasts were recorded "as is." Students were able to re-record when they didn't like their opening statements or if they messed up a few lines; long pauses were eliminated and sound effects were added later. Once students watched the technology specialist and I use Audacity, they quickly got the hang of it and were able to edit their own podcasts.

Assessment and Standards Addressed

Assessment

Student podcasts were evaluated based on content, presentation, and collaboration of the partners on the podcast. This assignment was done completely during class time, although students could choose to work on it after school, as well. We created an evaluation rubric and included "Use of class time" in the rubric.

The podcasts were uploaded onto our class wiki as well as the school website. Students and parents were invited to listen to the engaging and informative audio content that our students had created.

Standards Addressed

ISTE Standards for Students (ISTE Standards•S)

Students used multiple literacies throughout the project, which allowed them to "demonstrate creative thinking and develop innovative products and processes using technology" (ISTE Standards•S, Creativity and Innovation). Students used "digital media and environments to communicate and work collaboratively" (ISTE Standards•S, Communication and Collaboration). Students used a variety of digital sources on the internet "to gather, evaluate, and use information" for their podcasts (ISTE Standards•S, Research and Information Fluency). Students used "critical-thinking skills to plan" and write and manage their podcast manuscripts (ISTE Standards•S, Critical Thinking, Problem Solving, and Decision Making). Students were acting as digital citizens contributing in a positive way (ISTE Standards•S, Digital Citizenship) to create unique podcasts that would be shared with a wider audience outside of our classroom walls. Lastly, students demonstrated "a sound understanding of technology concepts, systems, and operations" involved in creating their podcasts (ISTE Standards•S, Technology Operations and Concepts).

1. **Creativity and Innovation**

   Students demonstrate creative thinking, construct knowledge, and develop innovative products and processes using technology.

2. **Communication and Collaboration**

   Students use digital media and environments to communicate and work collaboratively, including at a distance, to support individual learning and contribute to the learning of others.

3. **Research and Information Fluency**

   Students apply digital tools to gather, evaluate, and use information.

4. **Critical Thinking, Problem Solving, and Decision Making**

   Students use critical-thinking skills to plan and conduct research, manage projects, solve problems, and make informed decisions using appropriate digital tools and resources.

5. **Digital Citizenship**

   Students understand human, cultural, and societal issues related to technology and practice legal and ethical behavior.

6. **Technology Operations and Concepts**

   Students demonstrate a sound understanding of technology concepts, systems, and operations.

Common Core State Standards for ELA: Anchor Standards

At the same time we were addressing technology standards, we were also addressing Common Core College and Career Readiness (CCR) Anchor Standards for reading, writing, speaking, and listening (www.corestandards.org/ELA-Literacy/CCRA/R).

The following CCR Anchor Standards were integrated into the Radiolab podcasting unit.

Reading

Integration of Knowledge and ideas

CCRA.R.7   Integrate and evaluate content presented in diverse media and formats, including visually and quantitatively, as well as in words.

Writing

Production and Distribution of Writing

CCRA.W.6   Use technology, including the internet, to produce and publish writing and to interact and collaborate with others.

Research to Build Present Knowledge

CCRA.W.7   Conduct short as well as more sustained research projects based on focused questions, demonstrating understanding of the subject under investigation.

CCRA.W.8   Gather relevant information from multiple print and digital sources, assess the credibility and accuracy of each source, and integrate the information while avoiding plagiarism.

Speaking and Listening

Comprehension and Collaboration

CCRA.SL.2   Integrate and evaluate information presented in diverse media and formats, including visually, quantitatively, and orally.

Presentation of Knowledge and Ideas

CCRA.SL.5   Make strategic use of digital media and visual displays of data to express information and enhance understanding of presentations.

Students' reading had a nonfiction emphasis, students conducted close studies of Radiolab podcasts, pulling out text-based evidence and reading for information, craft, and structure. Students researched to build present knowledge, wrote, and presented their knowledge and ideas via the podcast. Students worked collaboratively to present their knowledge and ideas. They also worked on style and craft.

Before receiving the assignment, students studied Radiolab's style and craft. The Common Core State Standards for English Language Arts College and Career Readiness Anchor Standards for Reading for 6–12 states (p. 35),

> To become college and career ready, students must grapple with works of exceptional craft and thought whose range extends across genres, cultures, … [that] serve as models for students' own thinking and writing. (www.corestandards.org/assets/CCSSI_ELA Standards.pdf)

I continually modeled elements of the project. Students were in continuous discussion with their classmates and project partner to extend their understanding of the Radiolab project.

Conclusion: Learning from the NPR Radiolab Model

The Radiolab model brought a creative twist to the traditional five-paragraph informative essay. Students explored topics that were of interest to them. The students' podcasts were informative, engaging, and rich with details. We even decided to share some of the podcasts on our class wiki. To hear some student podcasts, visit our class wiki at www.rmsspeechanddebate.wikispaces.com.

I strive for "authentic and technology-rich work that is meaningful and productive for students" (Vasinda & McLeod, 2011). The Radiolab show on NPR proved to be a highly effective model in providing this for my students.

References

International Society for Technology in Education (ISTE). (2007). *National educational technology standards for students (NETS•S)* (2nd ed.). Eugene, OR: Author. Retrieved from www.iste.org/standards/nets-for-students

National Governors Association Center for Best Practices, Council of Chief State School Officers. (2010). *Common Core State Standards for English language arts & literacy.* Washington, DC: National Governors Association Center for Best Practices. Retrieved from www.corestandards.org/the-standards and www.corestandards.org/assets/CCSSI_ELA%20Standards.pdf

Radiolab. Various Podcasts. Retrieved from www.radiolab.org/archive

Vasunda, S., & McLeod, J. (2011). Extending readers theatre: A powerful and purposeful match with podcasting. *The Reading Teacher, 64,* 7.

CHAPTER 12

Crafting an Argumentative Essay with Evernote

Troy Hicks

LEVEL

Grades 6–12 / Ages 11–18 / Middle and High School

TECHNOLOGY

Evernote

LITERACY

Crafting an argumentative essay

STANDARDS

ISTE Standards•S, Common Core ELA (Writing, *W*)

As any informed discussion of educational technology should, I want to begin by offering a vision of the ways in which our students can engage in literacy practices associated with new technologies. In this chapter we'll follow teacher Mrs. Smith and her eighth grade student, Samantha, as Samantha researches and writes an argumentative essay.

Mrs. Smith is a composite of many of the teachers with whom I've worked over the past 10 years as a teacher educator and professional development consultant, most recently as director of the Chippewa River Writing Project at Central Michigan University. She also represents the kind of teacher I aspired to be when I began in the middle school classroom about 15 years ago: one who aimed to use technology in engaging, smart ways. In this chapter, I describe how Mrs. Smith invites her students to craft an argumentative essay using the web-based tool Evernote (www.evernote.com) as a hub for information gathering in the context of changes brought about by the Common Core State Standards (CCSS).

Mrs. Smith's Digital Writing Workshop

In Mrs. Smith's eighth grade language arts classroom, students engage in a writing workshop similar to the models described by longtime advocates of the approach such as Lucy Calkins (1994), Nancie Atwell (1998), and Donald Graves and Penny Kittle (Graves & Kittle, 2005).

Smith collaborates with students, supporting them in pursuing their own interests. She tries to strike a balance between the tasks her district expects all students to do—reading pre-selected books and writing in particular genres—and the more authentic reading and creative writing that students like to do, especially when using computers.

To that end, she has become more fluent with professional resources that address adolescent literacy in a digital age (Kajder, 2010; Kist, 2009; DeVoss, Eidman-Aadahl, & Hicks, 2010), and is now working to create a "digital writing workshop" (Hicks, 2009) in her classroom. She wants students to use the mobile devices in their pockets, as well as other Web 2.0 technologies, to collect and organize research for an argumentative essay.

The Context for Writing with the Common Core State Standards

There are two significant changes to writing instruction and assessment that will become evident with the implementation of the CCSS. First, Calkins, Ehrenworth, and Lehman (2012) suggest that we will need to "[p]rioritize argument and informational writing" (p. 18).

Second, the assessments for the CCSS will likely rely on students creating formulaic essays to be composed on and scored by computers. However, to fully teach argumentative and informational writing, we must make sure that our students are not constrained to such limiting and limited forms of writing, especially when the tools of digital production are becoming more accessible.

The CCSS for writing, here quoted from the eighth grade section (CCSS. ELA-Literacy.W.8.6), states that students should use technology in generative ways to craft writing.

Common Core State Standards for ELA

Writing

Production and Distribution of Writing

W.8.6   Use technology, including the internet, to produce and publish writing and present the relationships between information and ideas clearly and efficiently as well as to interact and collaborate with others. (www.corestandards.org/ELA-Literacy/W/8/6)

This raises some key questions:

- As the standards move from a focus on narrative texts to one more on informational and argumentative texts, how do we still invite students to read and write in a variety of genres, for many purposes?

- How can we support traditional academic literacies while simultaneously engaging in multimedia authoring?

- How can teachers and students access online materials outside of school, using mobile devices and networked computers?

- And, perhaps, core to the entire discussion: What does it mean to be "literate" during this second decade of the 21st century?

The CCSS are not simply about using technology to support writing, but also a way to think about the particular qualities of writing as expressed through different genres. As noted in Hillocks' book *Teaching Argument Writing: Supporting Claims with Relevant Evidence and Clear Reasoning* (2011), two primary reasons for teaching students argumentative writing is so that they will engage in actual research, not just summarize secondary reports of others' research and so that they can move beyond the typical "learned solutions" to many of the school-based problems that they get year after year (p. 68). If argumentative writing is to be taught at all, it must be taught through inquiry and logic.

Throughout the entire unit of study described below, Mrs. Smith is guided by her understanding of the reading and writing workshop approach to teaching, her emerging understandings about argumentative writing, and what she knows will support her students as digital learners. Technology can, ideally, help students keep track of their thinking through this often messy process. Criteria for assessing their essays will be based on logical thinking and sound argument, not merely on the number of paragraphs or the emotional persuasion evident.

To that end, this chapter outlines the progress that one of her students, Samantha, makes by using Evernote in lieu of 3 × 5-inch notecards, pre-formatted outlines, and templates requiring a certain number of paragraphs. Throughout the process, Mrs. Smith integrates a workshop model of teaching—including mini-lessons on specific skills and conferring with individual writers—to guide her students towards their final products.

Beginning the Research Process with Evernote

Mrs. Smith invites her students, with their parents' permission, to create an account with Evernote and shows them the basics for setting up an Evernote notebook. More important, she has students share their notebooks with her, so she can actively stay engaged in the students' research process over the next few weeks by providing comments and feedback. She also suggests that students may download and install Evernote on their (or their parents') smart phones so they can keep track of information while on the go.

One of Mrs. Smith's students, Samantha, has taken a particular interest in her topic for her argumentative essay: global climate change. As students started their first notebook, Mrs. Smith asked them to capture some of their initial thinking by creating their first note. Very much in the spirit of a freewrite, she wants them to use this first note as a way to document the research experience over the next few weeks, adding to it as they see fit. (Figure 12.1)

Figure 12.1 The beginning of Samantha's Evernote notebook on climate change

Capturing Sources, Documenting the Process

The CCSS for argumentative writing are a shift for Mrs. Smith and her students. In the past, she taught essay writing with a "persuasive" lens, rather than an "argumentative" one. However, the standards now require writers to support their claims with substantial evidence and logic—the essence of argument—not merely appeals to emotion or superfluous examples. Thus, over the course of the next few days in class, they work to identify a number of websites that can be useful for gathering information about many sides of their issue, including ProCon.org and FactCheck.org. They talk about search terms, moving beyond just the top few hits provided by a search engine, how to assess a website's credibility, and ways that they can use Evernote's Web Clipper tool to document and annotate their sources.

For her first source, Samantha opens up a new tab in her web browser and goes directly to the Environmental Protection Agency's site about climate change. She uses the Web Clipper button that has been installed on her browser's toolbar to pull up an annotation window (Figure 12.2). Mrs. Smith has asked all of her students when they record a source to use a tag of either "Reliable Sources," (from experts), "Questionable Sources" (from websites that seem to contradict what the students know about the topic), or "Non-Expert Sources" (because she does want students to include information from their families, friends, and classmates).

Figure 12.2 Creating a web clipping from the EPA climate change site with the Evernote Web Clipper

For her second source, Samantha finds the Wikipedia entry on climate change and notices that there are some sections on additional reasons such as volcanism and plate tectonics listed there. Because she wants to capture some of the exact text from the website, she highlights it and then right clicks to pull up a contextual menu where she can "Clip the Selection to Evernote" (Figure 12.3). Because her teacher has talked with the entire class about Wikipedia and other sources such as blogs and discussion boards that can contain biased or false information, Samantha tags this as a "Questionable Source."

Samantha wants to make sure that things are going well with her Evernote notebook, so she clicks back over to the other tab and notices that both the EPA and Wikipedia entries have been saved (Figure 12.4). Before she forgets, she clicks on the arrow next to the notebook title and chooses to share it with Mrs. Smith.

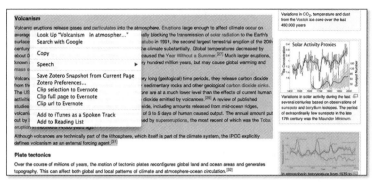

Figure 12.3 Right-clicking (control clicking) to use the Evernote Web Clipper on the Wikipedia page for climate change

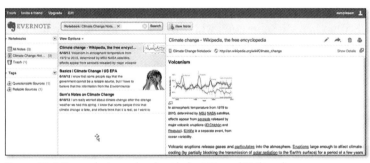

Figure 12.4 Samantha's notebook with the EPA and Wikipedia notes

Before the bell rings, Samantha thinks she has time to review one other source. She goes back to her search results and finds an entry from Forbes.com. Clicking on the link she discovers an interesting fact reported about a recent survey from the American Meteorological Society and how many of its members do not believe in global climate change. While she knows that Forbes.com should be a reliable source, she is also questioning the accuracy of this information and returns to her notebook. Underneath the web clipping, she changes the font color to red (Figure 12.5) and types in the following annotation: "I know that Forbes is a pretty reliable website and that they have a link in this article directly to the American Meteorological Society survey. Still, I find it kind of interesting that there is an ad for BP Oil right next to the text of this article."

Figure 12.5 Adding notes to the Forbes.com web clip

In the Field, Capturing Other Sources

As she continues to do her research, Samantha talks with a number of her class-mates as well as her mother. One afternoon while driving home from school, she and her mom begin a discussion about the issue of climate change. Realizing that her mother may not be a scientist but certainly has something to say about the topic, she asks if she can borrow her mom's iPhone. Quickly, she downloads the Evernote app, signs in, and then Samantha begins recording the conversation with her mother (Figure 12.6).

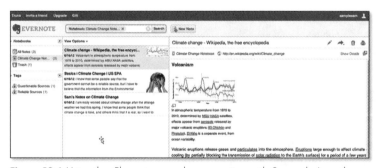

Figure 12.6 Using the iPhone to record conversation with Samantha's mother

When she arrives at home, Samantha logs in to her Evernote account, and again changes the font color on the note to add a brief annotation (Figure 12.7). Now that she is able to use her mom's iPhone as a recording device, she thinks she may try to do some other interviews with her family and friends to take an informal poll about their beliefs towards climate change. She will be able to use this data in her argumentative essay to show how local opinions about the topic are similar to or different from the experts and skeptics that she has been researching online.

Figure 12.7 The audio syncs to Samantha's notebook and she adds comments

Pulling Her Research Together

As her research continues, Samantha now has a variety of sources documented in her notebook. Because she has been conscientious throughout the process and has tagged each one as either "Reliable Sources," "Questionable Sources," or "Non-Expert Sources," she has quite a bit of information that she can put into the draft for her argumentative essay the next day in class.

As a way to help students get started with organizing their evidence, Mrs. Smith points them to ReadWriteThink.org as a resource, and suggests that the students create a working outline using the interactive "Persuasion Map" on the site. Students are able to copy and paste information from their Evernote notebook directly into this Flash-based tool, which then creates a one-page "map" of the main points for their essays. Students print out the essay map before they leave the computer lab that day, and will use it tomorrow in class to begin handwriting their rough drafts since computer time is limited. Mrs. Smith also quickly mentions the EasyBib site (www.easybib.com) because next week when they come back to type their final drafts, the students will also use it to format the citations for all the sources they already have documented in Evernote.

Assessment and Standards Addressed

Common Core State Standards for ELA

The project was guided by CCSS, in particular the ELA standard for Writing, W.8.6, which appeared earlier and is repeated here.

Writing

Production and Distribution of Writing

W.8.6   Use technology, including the internet, to produce and publish writing and present the relationships between information and ideas clearly and efficiently as well as to interact and collaborate with others. (www.corestandards.org/ELA-Literacy/W/8/6)

Students were engaged. Essays were completed. And now the real work begins for Mrs. Smith.

Throughout the entire unit of study, Mrs. Smith has been balancing Samantha's needs—as well as the needs of dozens of other students—with the goals that she has for the overall unit on argumentative writing. She has been guided by her understanding of the reading and writing workshop, as well as what she knows will support her students as digital learners. How—and in what ways—will she assess the process of researching, as well as the argumentative essays themselves? How has she helped her students build a repertoire of digital skills and literacy practices so that they can do smart work as writers?

Mrs. Smith's example helps us think about how to help students make decisions about which tools to use, when, and for which purposes. She does this in the context of crafting a traditional argumentative essay, combined with the ability for students to carefully identify and document a variety of sources. In the process, she guides students through a series of personal decisions about what they want to research and, more importantly, how they want to go about conducting and representing that research. While there may be others, I see in this example that Mrs. Smith is engaging her students in the following ISTE Standards for Students.

ISTE Standards for Students (ISTE Standards•S)

1. **Creativity and Innovation**

   Students demonstrate creative thinking, construct knowledge, and develop innovative products and processes using technology. Students:

   b.   create original works as a means of personal or group expression

2. **Communication and Collaboration**

   Students use digital media and environments to communicate and work collaboratively, including at a distance, to support individual learning and contribute to the learning of others. Students:

   a.   interact, collaborate, and publish with peers, experts, or others employing a variety of digital environments and media

   b.   communicate information and ideas effectively to multiple audiences using a variety of media and formats

6. **Technology Operations and Concepts**

   Students demonstrate a sound understanding of technology concepts, systems, and operations. Students:

   b.   select and use applications effectively and productively

Thus, Mrs. Smith sits down for her weekend of evaluating student work with a rubric that looks less like a checklist—"effective introduction," "strong thesis," "adequate examples"—and more like a tool to begin a conversation with her students. In some ways, this is really just a conclusion to the conversation that has been going on all along in their Evernote notebooks, especially with their free-writing. Mrs. Smith must take into account both the process and the product of the final argumentative essay.

Her criteria are shown in the following rubric (Form 12.1).

Essay (50%)	How well does the author define the problem and provide evidence? Represent all sides of the problem? In what ways does the author defend an appropriate solution to the problem?
Comments:	
Notebook (30%)	How well does the author choose media (websites, interviews, images, etc.) to support his/her argument without resorting to emotional appeals?
Comments:	

Form 12.1 Rubric for argumentative essay

Once she has provided some written comments as well as the final grade on the rubric, Mrs. Smith also goes in to Samantha's notebook to record a brief audio message describing the main points that she felt Samantha covered in her essay and complimenting her on the hard work she has done over the past few weeks. And, unlike the report card that will go home at the end of the term, Samantha was able to share this audio feedback immediately with her mom, who praises her as well.

References

Atwell, N. (1998). *In the middle: New understandings about writing, reading, and learning* (2nd ed.). Portsmouth, NH: Boynton/Cook.

Calkins, L., Ehrenworth, M., & Lehman, C. (2012). *Pathways to the Common Core: Accelerating achievement.* Portsmouth, NH: Heinemann.

Calkins, L. M. (1994). *The art of teaching writing.* Portsmouth, NH: Heinemann.

DeVoss, D., Eidman-Aadahl, E., & Hicks, T. (2010). *Because digital writing matters: Improving student writing in online and multimedia environments.* Hoboken, NJ: Jossey-Bass.

Graves, D. H., & Kittle, P. (2005). *Inside writing: How to teach the details of craft.* Portsmouth, NH: Heinemann.

Hicks, T. (2009). *The digital writing workshop.* Portsmouth, NH: Heinemann.

Hillocks, Jr., G. (2011). *Teaching argument writing, grades 6-12: Supporting claims with relevant evidence and clear reasoning.* Portsmouth, NH: Boynton/Cook.

Kajder, S. (2010). *Adolescents and digital literacies: Learning alongside our students.* Urbana, IL: National Council of Teachers of English.

Kist, W. R. (2009). *The socially networked classroom: Teaching in the new media age.* Thousand Oaks, CA: Corwin Press.

National Governors Association Center for Best Practices, Council of Chief State School Officers. (2010). *Common Core State Standards for English language arts & literacy.* Washington, DC: National Governors Association Center for Best Practices. Retrieved from www.corestandards.org/the-standards

ReadWriteThink.org. (n.d.). Persuasion Map—ReadWriteThink. Author. Retrieved from www.readwritethink.org/classroom-resources/student-interactives/persuasion-30034.html

Smekens Education Solutions. (2012). Argumentative v. persuasive writing. Retrieved from www.smekenseducation.com/argumentative-v-persuasive-writing.html

CHAPTER 13

Enhancing the Argument
Using Threaded Discussion as a Persuasive Prewriting Tool

Jason J. Griffith

LEVEL

Grade 8 / Ages 13–14 / Middle School

TECHNOLOGY

Edublogs

LITERACY

Persuasive writing

STANDARDS

ISTE Standards•S, Common Core ELA (Writing, W)

"I think we should get to go outside."

"Lunch period should be longer."

"We should be able to have our cell phones in class."

"It's not fair that we have to…"

My eighth graders love to argue and opine, so persuasive writing has always generated interest. However, when we've arrived at actually composing a persuasive essay, the passion for debate was often stifled by the traditional, two-dimensional print essay, a form that seemed to limit the positive interaction generated through live discussion. This was not surprising, because my student writers composed and published their essays in isolation. They'd select a topic, draft and refine an essay (sometimes with the help of a peer reviewer or two) and then turn it in for a grade. But these would be read by at most three other people, and in turn, each student was exposed to only the same small number of essays from other student writers.

Background

With the traditional persuasive essay, the arguments of my students were often unrefined, lacking in depth, and easily invalidated. It was not uncommon for students to make generalizations beginning with statements like "most people believe that …" which could easily be refuted by other students in discussion. Many times I reflected on how I could harness the energy from live discussion for more informed persuasive writing, as well as how I could offer students more exposure to each others' viewpoints.

After attending a workshop for teachers on blogging with the web-based resource Edublogs (www.edublogs.org), I had a potential solution. With Edublogs, teachers create personalized accounts to write and share blog entries with students who can then post comments and reply to each other in a threaded discussion (showing various layers of responses). Encouraging students to post and debate positions through comments and replies on issues presented in the blog posts would allow for just the sort of informed debate I was hoping for.

Teaching and Learning Persuasive Writing through Blogging

During our persuasive writing unit this year, I created seven blog posts on various debatable issues chosen by me and my classes. Then, I required students to choose and comment on two of these blog threads. Comments were to clearly state and defend a position on the selected issue in a well-developed paragraph. Students were also required to post two replies to each other's comments; replies could ask a question, offer a web resource, share an anecdote, respectfully refute an opinion, or confirm a position. After these threaded discussions had unfolded for about a week and a half, students chose one of their two positions from the threads to develop into a persuasive essay. This threaded discussion served as effective prewriting for the final essays. Because students had a chance to refine and defend their positions, receive feedback from me and their peers, read opposing viewpoints, and share resources and anecdotes, the resulting essays were more informed and featured better-defined and defended positions.

In the first step of this process, students selected screen names to identify themselves on their comments and replies. Requiring screen names was intended to protect their privacy since the Edublogs page would be viewable by anyone online. But the students found an added benefit; they really appreciated having mutual anonymity. As one student stated: "It was easier to express my opinions strongly when I didn't know who I was talking to." The screen names were very popular with students, in part, because they seemed to alleviate some of the pressure of social cliques.

Next, we chose issues to debate. After defining an issue (as a controversial topic) and a position (as an arguable statement about an issue), students brainstormed the issues that they were most interested in debating to generate an extensive list. Each of my four main class sections voted for one issue, and I also selected three of my favorites for a total of seven choices. The selected topics included the use of Facebook in education; the use of personal technology (cell phones, e-readers, etc.) in school; the benefits and drawbacks of reality television; no tolerance policies for school violence and weapons; the relevance of handwriting and cursive versus keyboarding and technology skills; the school locker policy, and access to backpacks and bags; and the length of the school day along with the school day schedule. After selecting these topics, I wrote a separate blog post briefly describing each issue and providing some initial web resources and articles. Then I opened the blogs to student comments.

Managing Online Conversations

Students were given roughly a week and a half to engage in the threaded discussions before moving on to drafting formal essays based on them. This time period included some class time as well as the encouragement to continue commenting outside of class. In this type of activity, it's important to consider students who may not have access to technology outside of school. In my case, the provided class time along with after school programs in our building allowed everyone the chance to participate and complete the assignment (during class times and in the evenings). I would review the comments and replies on each of the blogs (the user account page on Edublogs allows convenient ways to do this), and I would identify positive responses as well as negative ones.

Edublogs has customizable security settings that prevent any blatant vulgarity and flag suspicious comments before they go live on the site. However, students can still get away with posting immature, irrelevant, and/or suggestive comments. I did my best to turn these negative posts into teachable moments. Each day, I'd highlight some immature or inappropriate responses, discourage future ones like them, and then delete them. I'd also highlight positive interactions and encourage more of the same.

At the start of one class period, I encouraged the sharing of more personal anecdotes and pointed out some effective ones. The next day, I encouraged students to ask more questions to help one another sharpen and defend their positions. During the last student work period, I asked students to search for and share valid web resources and articles. I was impressed with how maturely and respectfully most of my students handled this activity while also getting into some pretty good discussion and debate.

When students completed both the prewriting threads and their resulting essays, I asked them for feedback in a short, reflective writing assignment. Out of 75 students who responded, 96% found the threaded discussion enjoyable, and 93% felt that the threads had helped to enhance their final essays. More specifically, a majority of students indicated that the threads had given them new ideas that they wouldn't have considered otherwise, helped them to identify their opposition, and provided them with helpful web resources. They liked that they were able to talk to students from other sections, that they could present their positions without being interrupted, and that everyone had a voice. While quiet students might not participate in a verbal debate, everyone contributed to this electronic one. The threads also offered a written record that students could refer back to; a verbal conversation might be forgotten, but they were able to repeatedly reference the threads as they drafted their essays.

Assessment

I assessed this project in a variety of ways. Of course, I comprehensively graded the final essays which needed to include elements from the threaded discussion (a clearly identified position, support from valid sources, identifying and overcoming opposition, etc.). Students provided written feedback on the effectiveness of the activity through the reflective writing activity. I also graded the comments and replies on the threaded discussion themselves. I gave credit for making the required number of posts, and I also had a content and grammar component for each to encourage students to post well-written responses.

In a more formative fashion, the threaded discussion itself allowed me to see students' viewpoints on the various issues expanding and developing. I made many specific replies to students myself, offering ideas for expansion, my own anecdotes, or helpful links and resources. By actively participating in the threads, I was able to give feedback to a greater number of students to help them improve their writing before I collected it (when the same type of feedback would have caused me to deduct points from the final essay).

The following student work samples show positive moments in two different threads, and paragraphs from the completed essays are shared as well. The first example (Figure 13.1) shows one student challenging another's perspective. The challenged student then ties in this opposition and attempts to overcome it in the final essay.

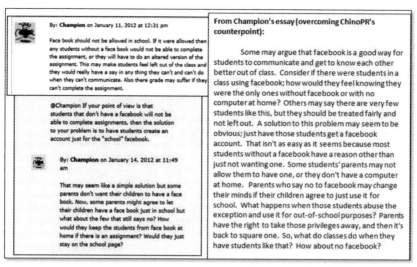

Figure 13.1 Work sample of a thread with one student challenging another's viewpoint

The second example (Figure 13.2) shows a student verifying the viewpoint of another on an issue. The student then tied some of the language from the verification into a body paragraph of the final essay.

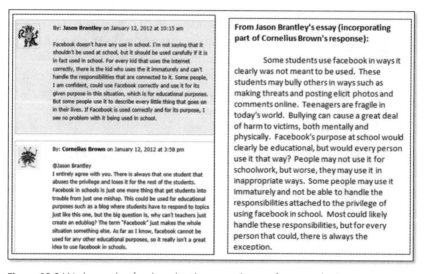

Figure 13.2 Work sample of a thread with one student verifying another's viewpoint

Even though I designed this activity for my eighth grade English language arts classes, I could see threaded discussion being used in a similar fashion across many grade levels and content areas. Certainly, prewriting strategies for a variety of modes could be enhanced through threads and adapted in complexity for younger or older students. Also, the potential exists for using threaded discussion in response to literature; it would be interesting to post various open-ended thematic questions based on assigned and chosen readings, and to allow students to explore and debate these through threads.

Besides Edublogs, there are many other free and paid platforms which allow for threaded discussion. Google's Blogger (www.blogger.com) offers free accounts, and our district uses paid SchoolWorld (www.schoolworld.com) template websites, which have a limited blog/discussion feature. We also use My Big Campus (www.mybigcampus.com), which mimics features of Facebook, Twitter, and other social media, including threaded discussion, in a closed educational network. A closed network like My Big Campus offers greater accountability as students have to sign in to use it, but the benefits of screen names and anonymity is sacrificed. One benefit of Edublogs is the comment layers shown within a thread. Some platforms feature only one layer of a thread (so all replies show up indiscriminately under a comment), but Edublogs layers responses to replies separately from replies to original comments, creating a more complex discussion.

Standards Addressed

ISTE Standards for Students (ISTE Standards•S)

Using threaded discussion for prewriting also supports several of the ISTE Standards for Students.

2. **Communication and Collaboration**

    Students use digital media and environments to communicate and work collaboratively, including at a distance, to support individual learning and contribute to the learning of others. Students:

    a. interact, collaborate, and publish with peers, experts, or others employing a variety of digital environments and media

    b. communicate information and ideas effectively to multiple audiences using a variety of media and formats

c.   develop cultural understanding and global awareness by engaging with learners of other cultures

Common Core State Standards

This activity supports several of the Common Core State Standards for ELA, Writing. Here are a few examples from Grade 8.

Writing

Text Types and Purposes

W.8.1   Write arguments to support claims with clear reasons and relevant evidence

- Introduce claim(s), acknowledge and distinguish the claim(s) from alternate or opposing claims, and organize the reasons and evidence logically.

- Support claim(s) with logical reasoning and relevant evidence, using accurate, credible sources and demonstrating an understanding of the topic or text.

Production and Distribution of Writing

W.8.6   Use technology, including the internet, to produce and publish writing and present the relationships between information and ideas clearly and efficiently as well as to interact and collaborate with others.

Conclusion

The experience of using threaded discussion as prewriting yielded positive benefits; I agree with my students who said that this activity greatly enhanced their writing. The set of essays that resulted was collectively the best written of the year. I will definitely continue to use strategies like this. I also plan to explore using a blog platform as a way for students to display and respond to each other's completed essays in the future, continuing to use technology to expand the audience for student writing.

Resources

Edublogs (www.edublogs.org) offers a free basic account that allows teachers to post blogs and students to submit comments and replies. There are also upgrades available (for yearly subscription fees) that provide more storage space and enhanced user features.

Screenr (www.screenr.com) Screenr allows users to record free screencasts and upload them to YouTube and social media. In order to better exhibit highlights and examples from this activity, I've recorded two screencasts using Screenr and then uploaded them to a channel on YouTube.

Enhancing the Argument—Part 1 (http://youtu.be/t9SiGpqiXBM)
The first video I uploaded to YouTube (Part 1) focuses on how I set up my blog posts, how students comment, active moderation of the threads, and some of the pitfalls that I encountered while conducting this activity.

Enhancing the Argument—Part 2 (http://youtu.be/rZL0Mw2Jfyw)
The second video (Part 2) shows specific examples of the benefits of using threaded discussion for persuasive prewriting as well as the connection between successful threaded discussion and its result in completed essays and assessment.

CHAPTER 14

Building Literacy with Popular Web 2.0 Tools

Sheryl R. Abshire, Cynthia D. Cummings,
Diane R. Mason, and L. Kay Abernathy

LEVEL

Grades K–12 / Ages 5–18 / Elementary, Middle, and High School

TECHNOLOGIES

Blogging, Edmodo, Wordle, Audacity

LITERACY

Reading and writing of journals and persuasive essays, reading aloud

STANDARDS

ISTE Standards•S, Common Core ELA (Writing, *W*, and Reading: Informational Text and Foundation Skills, *RI* and *RF*)

B logs, Edmodo, Wordle, and Audacity, oh, my! The engaging and stimulating world of Web 2.0 has become a standard in many classrooms of today. But what is Web 2.0 and why should we care?

O'Reilly (2005) reported that the use of the term Web 2.0 became popular, initially, as a way to describe business models and trends that were sustained beyond the tech sector crash of the 1990s. The things that survived were similar in several ways: They tended to be collaborative, interactive, and dynamic. Essentially, the users were consuming content and creating it simultaneously. However, today Web 2.0 is recognized not as a web only of text, but rather a web of multisensory communication.

The K–12 world has become a huge consumer of dynamic user-centered Web 2.0 resources. Visit a progressive K–12 classroom today, and you are likely to see a wealth of Web 2.0 resources being used across subject areas. Blogs, wikis, podcasts, VoiceThread, Wordle, Penzu, Twitter, and Evernote are but a sample of the thousands of Web 2.0 resources available to students and teachers to create an engaged interactive learning environment. King (2011) observed that students' culture has dramatically changed, and in order to align with their world, educators have altered their pedagogical approaches. These new pedagogical approaches are student-centered and are in response to the cultural and literacy demands of the information age. Solomon and Schrum (2007) defined literacy today as "acquiring new skills, including those of using technology, understanding science, having global awareness, and most important, having the ability to keep learning" (p. 20). Consequently, we have seen huge strides made in contributing to the growth of literacy with the use of Web 2.0 tools.

Educators are constantly seeking new solutions to engage learners in dynamic, authentic learning activities. Web 2.0 tools can be the answer. By engaging students with motivating digital tools, teachers often can see huge gains not only in basic literacy, but also in overall learning. This chapter will highlight four excellent examples of Web 2.0 tools used in innovative ways to expand literacy opportunities for students across grade levels and subject areas. These four snapshots illustrate how these uses play out in actual classroom implementation.

Blogging to Support Struggling Writers

Ashleigh Schulz, fifth grade teacher in the Calcasieu Parish Public Schools in Lake Charles, Louisiana, swears by the use of blogs in her classroom. A blog is often a personal journal published on the internet consisting of discrete entries or posts. The entries are typically displayed in reverse chronological order with the most recent first. Blogs can be the work of a single individual or of a small group. As teacher leader and model technology teacher in the school system, Schulz has hosted technology leaders from around the country in her classroom. The author works with her extensively on numerous technology-enabled projects and regularly observes her classroom as part of varied professional development scenarios.

Schulz contends the use of blogs expand and extend the possibilities and capabilities of K–12 literacy instruction by providing opportunities for students to gain understanding of print and electronic text. The main setting for this practice is the classroom, but it is easily carried over by students into their home lives with internet access.

The effects of utilizing blogs in the classroom have been nothing but positive! Students initially functioning below grade level are now excelling in the area of language arts. A particularly compelling example involves a struggling fifth grade student functioning at second grade level. By using classroom blogs, the teacher was able to tap into the student's unrecognized strengths. New blog topics were presented weekly to the class in the form of a sample constructed response item (open-ended question). Initially, the student was unable to answer the questions independently, but was able to grow on her own through critiquing other students' posts, thus learning where she was going wrong in her own posts. This, in turn, strengthened her ability to answer constructed response questions as well as strengthened her ability to communicate verbally and through electronic text. The student went on to be a finalist in an essay competition that was shared with all of the school's fifth grade classes. She also had a writing sample featured in the local newspaper. Although she sometimes had trouble with subject-verb agreement, she was able to push through her errors and enhance her own learning by noticing areas of weakness in other students' blog posts. This student would often work from home because she loved to help the other students. A student who was often shy and not extremely social saw her voice grow into that of a literate student through the power of blogging.

Blogging can initially be introduced as a whole class activity. Since blogging is often new to students when they begin the school year, a suggested activity is to take them to the computer lab and walk them through the basic how-tos of blogging. After an initial trial period, a few experts will emerge who will be the "go-to" students if problems arise. For the most part, utilizing blogs as an individual assignment and as part of group rotations within the classroom is very successful. Although the actual assignment is individual, the critiquing or "comments" become a collaborative effort within the class.

Students rotate through stations on a daily basis, one of which is the blog station. This approach is easily achievable with a small number of classroom computers. The goal is to have each student blog at some point throughout each week, assigning meaningful technology-related tasks that enhance the curriculum. Today's students are technology proficient. The act of blogging can tap into their varying ability levels to produce work that far exceeds what would traditionally be obtained through a pencil and paper exercise. Expectations on all constructed response test items include: turning around the question (restating the question), answering the question correctly and completely, and finally proving the answer with specific details from class literature, lessons, or wherever information was gained. These expectations are outlined in a rubric that is presented to the students at the beginning of the year. Student work is assessed using running records as well as posting suggestions and comments to the individual blog posts.

The practice of using blogs to enhance literacy in the curriculum can be applied to any student population. The practice works successfully with low performing students, average students, as well as advanced level learners. In PK, students could blog with the teacher to keep a class blog about what is going on in their classroom. This exposure to blogging could be a catalyst to enhance literacy as a whole. In higher grade levels, students could begin writing sentences, then paragraphs to build literacy and communication through electronic text. The sky's the limit with posing questions that push students far beyond the basic who, what, when, where, why, and how.

All that is required to begin blogging with students is to have basic computer access and an internet connection. While there are numerous paid blogging sites, Schulz uses the internal blogging tools in Blackboard, but a vast supply of free blogging sites exist, such as Blogger (www.blogger.com), WordPress (www.wordpress.org), Weebly (www.weebly.com), and LiveJournal (www. livejournal.com). More free blogging tool recommendations can be found at http://mashable.com/2007/08/06/free-blog-hosts.

How To Use Blogger

One of the simple, commonly used, free blogging resources the author recommends for teachers is Google's Blogger. The following are informational resources about using Blogger.

Google in Education Blogger page: www.google.com/edu/resources/blogger.html
This provides a valuable overview of the Blogger resource and its suitability as a classroom resource with links to more information of value.

Blogger "Getting Started" page: www.blogger.com/features#gettingStarted
This has good descriptions of the features this blogging resource offers for beginners.

How to Create a Blog on Blogger: www.youtube.com/watch?v=rA4s3wN_vK8
This video tutorial is easy to understand and follow.

Standards Addressed

Common Core State Standards for ELA

Writing

Text Types and Purposes

W.4.1 Write opinion pieces on topics or texts, supporting a point of view with reasons and information.

W.4.2 Write informative/explanatory texts to examine a topic and convey ideas and information clearly.

W.4.3 Write narratives to develop real or imagined experiences or events using effective technique, descriptive details, and clear event sequences.

Production and Distribution of Writing

W.4.4 Produce clear and coherent writing in which the development and organization are appropriate to task, purpose, and audience. (Grade-specific expectations for writing types are defined in standards 1–3 above.)

W.4.5 With guidance and support from peers and adults, develop and strengthen writing as needed by planning, revising, and editing.

W.4.6   With some guidance and support from adults, use technology, including the internet, to produce and publish writing as well as to interact and collaborate with others; demonstrate sufficient command of keyboarding skills to type a minimum of one page in a single sitting.

Research to Build Present Knowledge

W.4.7   Conduct short research projects that build knowledge through investigation of different aspects of a topic.

W.4.8   Recall relevant information from experiences or gather relevant information from print and digital sources; take notes and categorize information, and provide a list of sources.

W.4.9   Draw evidence from literary or informational texts to support analysis, reflection, and research.

Range of Writing

W.4.10   Write routinely over extended time frames (time for research, reflection, and revision) and shorter time frames (a single sitting or a day or two) for a range of discipline-specific tasks, purposes, and audiences.

ISTE Standards for Students (ISTE Standards•S)

1. **Creativity and Innovation**

   Students demonstrate creative thinking, construct knowledge, and develop innovative products and processes using technology.

2. **Communication and Collaboration**

   Students use digital media and environments to communicate and work collaboratively, including at a distance, to support individual learning and contribute to the learning of others.

3. **Research and Information Fluency**

   Students apply digital tools to gather, evaluate, and use information.

4. **Critical Thinking, Problem Solving, and Decision Making**

   Students use critical-thinking skills to plan and conduct research, manage projects, solve problems, and make informed decisions using appropriate digital tools and resources.

5. **Digital Citizenship**

   Students understand human, cultural, and societal issues related to technology and practice legal and ethical behavior.

6. **Technology Operations and Concepts**

   Students demonstrate a sound understanding of technology concepts, systems, and operations.

Fostering Collaboration in Literacy Learning with Edmodo

Edmodo is an online learning platform that promotes anytime, anyplace learning. Functionally, it allows teachers to post messages, discuss classroom topics, assign and grade classwork, share content and materials, and network and exchange ideas with their peers. Michelle LaRue, a sixth grade English language arts teacher in a Lumberton, Texas, middle school uses Edmodo to provide opportunities for her students to be 21st-century readers and writers through the use of multimedia projects. The author provided technology consultation for several years in the school where LaRue works, and has had an opportunity to observe and work with her regarding the use of technology integration. One of these projects was a persuasive research/video project where students used Web 2.0 tools such as Edmodo, Animoto, interactive graphic organizers, collaborative videoconferencing, word processing, and vozMe.

The purpose of the project was for students to individually plan, write, and edit a persuasive essay on a topic they selected. Once students created their essays, they were placed in groups of common topics. The groups of two to three students compared their essays and determined the three most important main ideas and supporting details. The groups created a video that was uploaded to Edmodo for sharing. Students then participated in a videoconference with a sixth grade class in Roseville, Michigan.

The project engaged and empowered students to actively participate in the reading and writing process. Students responded positively to the use of technology and the ease of planning, editing, and finalizing their essays. Students eagerly collaborated with their peers in an online community. They became responsible for their own learning and provided support to their peers. Presenting their work to an authentic audience served as a catalyst for students to produce products with more in-depth content than in traditional classrooms. Students were conscious of the need to find and report valid and appropriate information.

The project began with whole group instruction on how to conduct an internet search for resources for the students' essays and how to log on to the Edmodo account. Students were provided four topics that they could choose to research: Should students vote? Should cell phones be used in the classroom? Should school be year-round? Should students be required to wear school uniforms? Links to resources on each topic were accessible in Edmodo. Students could upload and share links they found during their own research. In order to provide access to articles for students with special needs, vozMe was used. vozMe is a simple online "text to speech" program that lets you enter any English or Spanish text and then play it as an audio stream. The teacher was able to post the articles to vozMe, convert the articles to an MP3 and upload the audio file to Edmodo with a copy of the article. This allowed the students with special needs to interact in online discussions with other students and to have equitable access to resources.

After selecting their topics and conducting their research, students organized their findings using an interactive digital graphic organizer to map their arguments for a persuasive essay or debate. Students organized their information to include an introduction, main idea, supporting details, and a conclusion. The finished organizer could be saved, emailed, or printed. Students then converted this to an outline in a word processing document. This outline was uploaded to Edmodo.

Using their outlines, students wrote persuasive essays and uploaded their final text-based essay to Edmodo. Students were placed in groups according to topic. Each student group compared their findings and determined what they considered the three most important ideas with supporting details. Next, they created a video using Animoto, a web application that produces videos from photos, video clips, and music. Students posted their videos to Edmodo for sharing with others. In a collaborative project with a sixth grade classroom in Roseville, Michigan, LaRue's students presented a three-minute debate on their issue. Students in the Roseville classroom voted for the most persuasive speech. Furthermore, students in each of the classrooms engaged in a discussion of the four topics and recognized the commonality of their opinions.

The main resources required for this simple but powerful project are a computer and internet access. Students will also need an Animoto account (www.animoto.com) and an Edmodo account (www.edmodo.com). These accounts provide secure sites for students to connect and collaborate, share content, and access class discussions and resources. The beauty of using Edmodo is that teachers can create an educator account and receive 50 free student accounts.

Other resources include a persuasive interactive graphic organizer available on the ReadWriteThink website (www.readwritethink.org/classroom-resources/student-interactives/persuasion-30034.html) and vozMe (www.vozme.com), a free online tool that offers applications and services to convert text into speech.

In terms of assessment, formative assessment is provided with the graphic organizer and an outline, and the summative assessment is the final persuasive essay, Animoto video, and the video conference presentation.

An example of student work may be viewed at http://animoto.com/play/eK0I8g1HBaB28ArI91FZSA.

How To Use Edmodo

Edmodo Frequently Asked Questions: https://support.edmodo.com/home#faq
This Edmodo resource is a great place to start.

Help Topics for Teachers: http://help.edmodo.com
This is Edmodo's web page of informational links for educators. Here you'll find vital information on getting started and other topics.

How to use vozMe: www.vozme.com
vozMe requires no learning to use; simply enter text and click on the Create MP3 button.

Standards Addressed

Common Core State Standards

Writing

Text Types and Purposes

W.6.1   Write arguments to support claims with clear reasons and relevant evidence.

Production and Distribution of Writing

W.6.4   Produce clear and coherent writing in which the development, organization, and style are appropriate to task, purpose, and audience.

W.6.5   With some guidance and support from peers and adults, develop and strengthen writing as needed by planning, revising, editing, rewriting, or trying a new approach.

W.6.6   Use technology, including the internet, to produce and publish writing as well as to interact and collaborate with others; demonstrate sufficient command of keyboarding skills to type a minimum of three pages in a single sitting.

Research to Build Present Knowledge

W.6.7   Conduct short research projects to answer a question, drawing on several sources and refocusing the inquiry when appropriate.

W.6.8   Gather relevant information from multiple print and digital sources; assess the credibility of each source; and quote or paraphrase the data and conclusions of others while avoiding plagiarism and providing basic bibliographic information for sources.

W.6.9   Draw evidence from literary or informational texts to support analysis, reflection, and research.

Range of Writing

W.6.10   Write routinely over extended time frames (time for research, reflection, and revision) and shorter time frames (a single sitting or a day or two) for a range of discipline-specific tasks, purposes, and audiences.

Reading: Informational Text

Integration of Knowledge and Ideas

RI.6.7   Integrate information presented in different media or formats (e.g., visually, quantitatively) as well as in words to develop a coherent understanding of a topic or issue.

RI.6.8   Trace and evaluate the argument and specific claims in a text, distinguishing claims that are supported by reasons and evidence from claims that are not.

Range of Reading and Level of Text Complexity

RI.6.10   By the end of the year, read and comprehend literary nonfiction in the grades 6–8 text complexity band proficiently, with scaffolding as needed at the high end of the range.

ISTE Standards for Students (ISTE Standards•S)

2.   Communication and Collaboration

Students use digital media and environments to communicate and work collaboratively, including at a distance, to support individual learning and contribute to the learning of others.

3.   Research and Information Fluency

Students apply digital tools to gather, evaluate, and use information.

Stimulating Interest in and Analysis of Writing with Wordle

Wordle (www.wordle.net) is a creative web-based application that transforms text such as essays and reports into word designs. It is an easy to use, online "word art engine" which produces attractive word clouds. Wordle provides ways to expand and extend K–12 literacy instruction. Students in Terri Simpson's seventh grade Maplewood Middle School English language arts classroom use Wordle for visual analysis of their writing. Simpson's background as a model technology classroom teacher adept at working in a 1:1 laptop environment provides students the guidance and technology support to successfully integrate various technologies in

ELA. The author provided technology professional development to Simpson at the district level, taught her in a graduate course, and observed her implementation of Wordle. Students in this Sulphur, Louisiana, classroom are able to see and recognize over-usage of specific words and assess the level of vocabulary in their writing using Wordle as a tool.

Wordle helps students to advance their writing techniques, leading to stronger essay completion. The seventh graders' motivation for writing improved. The classroom teacher reported Wordle is an exciting tool that elevates the possibilities and capabilities of ELA instruction for K–12 teachers.

Implementing this project began with the teacher demonstrating how to copy and paste essays into the online Wordle creator. Initially the teacher performed a basic demonstration of how to alter color choices, orientation, and printing options as a whole group. Then Wordle was used to compare and alter word choice as an individual or team process. Each student self-analyzed their writing and made adjustments based on feedback from their team members. This Web 2.0 tool can be used to model and share improved writing samples with individuals, small groups, large groups, or collaboratively with another audience.

Classroom teachers can easily implement Wordle as a tool and strategy to stimulate writing interest and self-analysis skills by permitting students to display their text in a word design. Students create their essays in Microsoft Word. Word features are used to check spelling and some grammar errors. The student copies and pastes the essay into the Wordle application. The result is a pictorial view of the essay enlarging the most frequently used words in what is termed a Wordle image. Overused words are enlarged. The more times the word appears in the essay, the larger it appears, which gives students a very visual approach to correction in their writing.

Students are then instructed to replace over-emphasized words with synonyms. The student changes the words in the original essay and reposts to Wordle. This process can be repeated as often as necessary. Next, students post their essays to the school's Holt Online Essay Scoring application to determine a score. Essays are scored from U (unscoreable) to 4 (well done). The classroom goal for this setting is to obtain a 4. Accommodations are made for students based on their individual needs, but even the special needs students are reported to be obtaining 4s.

Student work is shared through posting of both excellent essays and the Wordles (word clouds) that were created. Students can post the Wordles in their digital portfolios, share with others online, and/or print them to keep and share. Student essays produced as a result of participation in the use of Wordle are stronger than prior to its use. The practice also appears to encourage more use of and knowledge about informational resources, such as a thesaurus, throughout the process of writing.

This practice could be utilized from Grade 4 up. Students assess their own writing, so no determination is placed on level of ability, just the reduction of redundancy. The teacher needs to give consideration to the number of accessible computers, internet service, and monitoring abilities. The required resources include internet access, a computer or device with Microsoft Word or other word processing software, and access to the Wordle site (www.wordle.net).

Students are required to submit one genre essay per grading period. They must edit, revise, and resubmit the writing piece. The formative assessment process involves multiple submissions that provide opportunities for the teacher to assess progress and redirect any misconceptions or erroneous practices. The summative assessment process grades students on the final draft of each essay (not all revisions) based on the Louisiana Writing Rubric for iLEAP, which ties this exercise directly to standardized high stakes assessments performed each spring. The essay portion of the Louisiana high stakes test mirrors these assignments, so students are quite comfortable with the writing portion of the test. Students in this classroom averaged 10 out of 12 points on the writing portion of the test, which showed an increased average of two points from the previous year.

How to Use Wordle

Wordle Home Page: www.wordle.net
Wordle is free and so easy to use that there is virtually nothing to learn. Once you are on this resources' website, its only direction is "Paste in a bunch of text."

Wordle Frequently Asked Questions: www.wordle.net/faq
Once you start using Wordle, you'll want to know a good deal of information about its finer points. These FAQs make that very, very easy.

Standards Addressed

Common Core State Standards

Writing

Text Types and Purposes

W.7.1 Write arguments to support claims with clear reasons and relevant evidence.

W.7.2 Write informative/explanatory texts to examine a topic and convey ideas, concepts, and information through the selection, organization, and analysis of relevant content.

W.7.3 Write narratives to develop real or imagined experiences or events using effective technique, relevant descriptive details, and well-structured event sequences.

Production and Distribution of Writing

W.7.4 Produce clear and coherent writing in which the development, organization, and style are appropriate to task, purpose, and audience.

W.7.5 With some guidance and support from peers and adults, develop and strengthen writing as needed by planning, revising, editing, rewriting, or trying a new approach, focusing on how well purpose and audience have been addressed.

W.7.6 Use technology, including the internet, to produce and publish writing and link to and cite sources as well as to interact and collaborate with others, including linking to and citing sources.

ISTE Standards for Students (ISTE Standards•S)

1. **Creativity and Innovation**

    Students demonstrate creative thinking, construct knowledge, and develop innovative products and processes using technology.

3. **Research and Information Fluency**

    Students apply digital tools to gather, evaluate, and use information.

4. **Critical Thinking, Problem Solving, and Decision Making**

    Students use critical-thinking skills to plan and conduct research, manage projects, solve problems, and make informed decisions using appropriate digital tools and resources.

6. **Technology Operations and Concepts**

    Students demonstrate a sound understanding of technology concepts, systems, and operations.

Promoting Reading Fluency with Audacity

Dawn Kirkland, a second grade Title I teacher in the Houston, Texas, area uses Audacity (http://audacity.sourceforge.net) as an essential element of reading fluency practice. The free, cross-platform software for recording and editing sounds allows students to record their reading efforts and become aware of their verbal strengths as well as areas where they need more work. Kirkland's district asked her to demonstrate use of the program to national visitors when the National School Board Association hosted one of their annual technology visits.

At this meeting, the author observed Kirkland and her students. The students record and save their readings as they learn and build self awareness. The teacher meets with the reading groups and is able to frequently assess all students. She accesses student network folders to assess the need for differentiated instruction. This process provides artifacts to determine the need for possible further interventions. She shares reading passages and stories with students so they can hear fluent reading and learn to appreciate the written word in many ways.

Students work at tables in their classrooms using headphones, microphones, desktop computers, and laptop computers with Audacity software. Initially, teachers provided small quiet areas for students to work on fluency skills. However, teachers discovered that privacy was not needed because students were so intently focused. It was determined that the microphones picked up the students' own voices with no interference from other students' voices near them.

Student learning has increased tremendously as a result. They are engaged in reading and timing their work while they view the strategy as a "game." Amazingly, students now beg to read! This enthusiasm for reading did not occur before they began this practice. Struggling readers experienced a significant boost in self-confidence. Using Audacity has resulted in a new school culture of support and encouragement. This program is used both by the classroom teacher and the reading specialists.

Using Audacity for recording, timing (rates), and listening to their own reading is an individual activity. The students do like to share their progress and that is encouraged, although they are discouraged from sharing their fluency rates. Stations are set up for individual students with an assessment for self-checking as well as for individual accountability.

Each week students begin with a fresh reading sample and recording. They each read twice on Mondays and then one more time on Tuesdays. After the teacher has listened and evaluated the readings, group time is planned according to needs. On Fridays students go back and reread a final time or two if they want. They then record the title of their book and each one of their times so that all readings and progress is monitored.

Students save their work to the district network, and the teacher analyzes and shares with reading specialists when necessary. In addition, the campus is implementing a new readers' theater at the end of each nine weeks. The reading groups prepare and record their reader's theater to share with the grade level. The files are posted on a password-protected page on each teacher's website so other classes may listen to the work.

This special practice is particularly effective with students from low socioeconomic populations and ELL students. Many of the students impacted are working below grade level. Students in these second grade classrooms use Audacity free software, desktop computers, headphones, and microphones.

For participation assessment, all students write in the station folder each day what activity they did and one piece of information about that day's work. For formative assessment, the teacher observes and analyzes the station work including the Audacity reading files. For summative assessment, students are tested on fluency twice during a nine-week grading period.

How to Use Audacity

Home page for Audacity: http://audacity.sourceforge.net
>Here you'll find links for free downloads of this software.

Wiki for Audacity: http://wiki.audacityteam.org/wiki/
Audacity_Wiki_Home_Page
>The wiki has additional links to manuals, help, tips, and so forth.

Forum for Audacity: http://forum.audacityteam.org
>This is the place for discussions among users.

How to Use Audacity: www.wikihow.com/Use-Audacity
>This is an excellent beginner's tutorial that explains how to record, play back, edit, and more with this powerful piece of free software.

Standards Addressed

Common Core State Standards

Reading: Foundational Skills

Phonics and Word Recognition

RF.2.3   Know and apply grade-level phonics and word analysis skills in decoding words.

Fluency

RF. 2.4   Read with sufficient accuracy and fluency to support comprehension.

ISTE Standards for Students (ISTE Standards•S)

1. **Creativity and Innovation**

   Students demonstrate creative thinking, construct knowledge, and develop innovative products and processes using technology.

2. **Communication and Collaboration**

   Students use digital media and environments to communicate and work collaboratively, including at a distance, to support individual learning and contribute to the learning of others.

4. **Critical Thinking, Problem Solving, and Decision Making**

   Students use critical-thinking skills to plan and conduct research, manage projects, solve problems, and make informed decisions using appropriate digital tools and resources.

Conclusion

It comes as no surprise to progressive, tech-savvy educators that Web 2.0 tools have become essential to strengthening literacy in today's classrooms. Research informs us that students today need a different set of literacy skills to live and learn in the 21st century (Gee, 2009; Jenkins, Clinton, Purushotma, Robison, & Weigel, 2006; Jones-Kavalier & Flannigan, 2008; Palfrey & Gasser, 2008; Partnership for 21st Century Skills, 2004). In *Literacy in the New Media Age,* Kress (2003) shared that technology was the logical choice to deliver a superior level of multimodal production. He contended traditional books cannot deliver in this manner and afford similar production and interpretation of sound, image, and print through music, graphics, and interactive text.

Therefore, the advances in the use of the internet—real-time information, virtual environments, and global knowledge connections—could strengthen communication and comprehension, and in due course, change literacy. Solomon and Schrum (2007) predicted that "using collaboration and communication tools with educational methods that also promote these skills—such as project-based learning—will help students acquire the abilities they need for the future" (p. 18).

References

Gee, J. P. (2009). Big thinkers: James Paul Gee on grading with games [video]. Retrieved from www.edutopia.org/digital-generation-james-gee-video

Jenkins, H., Clinton, K., Purushotma, R., Robison, A., & Weigel, M. (2006). *Confronting the challenges of participatory culture: Media education for the 21st century.* Chicago, IL: The MacArthur Foundation. Retrieved from http://files.eric.ed.gov/fulltext/ED536086.pdf

Jones-Kavalier, B., & Flannigan, S. (2008). Connecting the digital dots: literacy of the 21st century. *EDUCAUSE Quarterly, 29*(2), 1–3.

King, R. (2011). Metacognition: Information literacy and web 2.0 as an instructional tool. *Currents in Teaching and Learning, 3*(2), 22–32.

Kress, G. (2003). *Literacy in the new media age.* London, UK: Routledge.

O'Reilly, T. (2005). *What is web 2.0: Design patterns and business models for the next generation of software.* Retrieved from www.oreillynet.com/pub/a/oreilly/tim/news/2005/09/30/what-is-web-20.html

Palfrey, J., & Gasser, U. (2008). *Born digital: Understanding the first generation of digital natives.* New York, NY: Basic Books.

Partnership for 21st Century Skills. (2004). *The intellectual and policy foundations of the 21st Century Skills Framework.* Retrieved from www.21stcenturyskills.org/route21/images/stories/epapers/skillsfoundationsfinal.pdf

Solomon, G., & Schrum, L. (2007). *Web 2.0: New tools, new schools.* Eugene, OR: International Society for Technology in Education.

SECTION V

and even more
INSPIRATION

CHAPTER 15

Literacy Growth through Digital Television News Production
    Grades 6–8 / Ages 11–14 / Middle School
    Digital video camera, Magix Movie Edit Pro (or other
    video editing software)

CHAPTER 16

Providing Feedback in the Writing Process with Digital Audio and Video
    Grades K–12 / Ages 5–18 / Elementary, Middle, and High School
    Vocaroo, Audioboo, Camtasia, Jing, Vimeo

CHAPTER 17

Using Online Vocabulary Resources
to Improve Pre-College ESL and SAT Literacy Skills
    Grades 10–12 / Ages 15–18 / High School
    Compleat Lexical Tutor

CHAPTER 18

Podcasting in Foreign Language Class
    Grades 6–8 / Ages 11–14 / Middle School
    Cell phone with recording capability, Audacity, GarageBand

Literacy Growth through Digital Television News Production

Angelo Carideo, Michael Downes,
and David Liotta

LEVEL

Grades 6–8 / Ages 11–14 / Middle School

TECHNOLOGIES

Digital video camera, Magix Movie Edit Pro
(or other video-editing software)

LITERACY

Video news production and broadcasting

STANDARDS

Common Core ELA (Reading: Literature, *RL*;
Writing, *W*; Speaking and Listening, *SL*;
and Language, *L*)

G ive them 22 minutes of early morning, school-wide television viewing time, and they'll give you the news! Twice a week before classes begin, students at Ditmas—I.S. 62, a public middle school in Brooklyn, New York—view a local television news show produced, starring, and written by their peers.

The Ditmas News Network (DNN) program is run by a team of self-nominated sixth to eighth grade students, including special needs, newcomer, English language learners, regular education, and enrichment learners. This team of 25 students is trained in basic reporting, researching primary and secondary sources, script development, digital still photography, sound, and video production as part of media/literacy efforts at the school.

DNN is one of the latest and most successful media production initiatives at a school that has a history of offering students opportunities for involvement in acting, script writing, digital videography and presenting social studies and language arts–related documentaries. These films have won multiple awards from the Chase Video Learning Contest and have been presented as part of the NYC local PBS/Channel 13–sponsored Celebration of Teaching & Learning annual conferences. You can take a look at our student news productions at www.ditmas.tv.

Beyond the Ditmas school audience of 1,300 middle school students, the teams have presented their work to diverse audiences around New York City, including Jewish parochial high school students, groups of adult voters, teen media film producers and actors at the Museum of the Moving Image, and teacher educators at York College. These presentations allow Ditmas student media producers to engage these audiences in face-to-face Q & A sessions about their work.

A Flexible Model

Viewed as a model for digital media production-driven literacy learning, the DNN approach can be replicated and integrated as part of a regular, Grade 6–8 ELA content class, or used in collaboration with social studies, science, or other content classes. The program could be modified for high school implementation as well, or offered as an after-school enrichment program specifically to support or enhance Common Core literacy learning or remedial objectives. The program might also be offered as a differentiated, project-based learning option for students in the context of the regular full class ELA program.

Not Just Fun Media Projects, but Effective Instructional Practice

The DNN program integrates ELA/Common Core (reading for informational text, RI; writing standards, W; speaking and listening standards, SL; and language, L, standards) into project-based activities. As part of this, students produce substantial text products—informational, persuasive, analytical, and creative writings and reports. They also practice speaking and listening skills.

This is accomplished through collaborative discussions to plan, research, investigate, conduct interviews for, and edit, their media end products. Completed products are posted online, a dynamic platform from which to showcase and share them. They also draw audience feedback in a way that is accessible and meaningful to the student creators.

We established the program because we realized the tremendous literacy and life-learning opportunities possible through the production of original student media products.

As Michael Downes puts it: "We are currently educating a new generation of visual learners. These students bring to our traditional English Language Arts, Social Studies, and other content area classes, their fascination with visual learning styles. When literacy educators tap into these rich media resources and digital media tools, we immediately make a captivating, real connection with content for our students."

David Liotta adds: "From my perspective as a literacy and social studies educator, the use of the media studio technique effectively involves students in opportunities to do project-based learning (in this case, authentic media products). As the students work together in media teams, they genuinely investigate, interview, examine, and critique real neighborhood, national, and global issues. They do this hands-on. For example, rather than just read local print and online news reports about school budgets, the current students involved in the Ditmas News Network actually went on site to interview Kensington, Brooklyn neighborhood adult residents about the closing of a local library branch. They videoed and later edited the actual neighborhood reaction to this budget cut. Tough 2011 local, economic times were concretized for Ditmas News Network I.S. 62 reporters when they stood in front of their favorite pizza shop and read the closing sign plus the posted notice about taxes owed by the shop."

Junior, a DNN eighth grader puts it this way:

> Being in this program has transformed the way I think and act. Before DNN, I didn't know what was going on around the school or the neighborhood. Frankly I didn't care. Then DNN came along and my job was to know what was going around, when and where. The best part of DNN was that I liked what I was doing and I was good at it.

Equipment Needs

While DNN student media productions reflect the supportive expertise of David and Angelo, the basic approach can be adapted and replicated in any middle school using any generally available equipment.

DNN uses a Sony HUR 1500 camera and the editing and production software Magix Movie Edit Pro. However, any digital camera and available video-editing production software will do for entry level adoptions of the approach.

Learning the Craft of Video News Production

The DNN program requires that students learn and apply the same skills necessary for real-world journalism. However, DNN students don't receive formal training in the use of cameras, sound, and editing software, nor in script development or on-camera presenting. Students learn from doing and from one another, and often from teacher modeling and demonstrations that arise from the needs experienced in the moment as the students put the shows together. As David likes to put it, "Just let the kids get a news story and start from there. They do two pilot runs before actually doing the show. It may look like chaos and disorder at first when the kids meet and discuss stories, but then the ongoing process of story selection, script development, and actual production of the news videos transforms that through focus and effort to ordered learning."

We recommend that students and teachers work together learning and refining their studio production skills as a team. Often, educators will find that the students are more expert at the studio media tools and learn more readily than their teachers. In that case, the teachers can focus on explicitly detailing Common Core literacy objectives.

Practice Primer

Step 1. Decide on a curriculum connection as the focus for your student news media products. Students in an ELA class could be asked to identify a broadcast news or online news story that connects with the informational or fictional texts they are studying.

Step 2. Be willing and ready to accept multiple student creative projects or approaches to your content product goal. Specifically, students may opt to poll peers or neighborhood passersby on the story or to editorialize an issue that it suggests.

Step 3. Present the product content goal to the students and allow at least one or two class periods for them to explore (individually or in small groups) the way they might approach it and how they might use the media tools to realize that approach.

Step 4. Follow the literacy writing workshop continuum in *Literacy: Helping Children Construct Meaning* (Cooper & Kiger, 2003). Teach the students how to work with media tools (have a student do the explanations if the student is more expert than the teacher). Then work with them individually or in small groups as they develop their initial media products and, finally, sit back as they present products they developed by themselves.

Step 5. Build in, through invitation and online offerings, focus audiences (which could be other teaching colleagues, partner school audiences online, and/or peer classes on school site) to provide feedback to the working student producers as they refine and edit their media work.

Step 6. Model for students, if necessary, how to conduct an interview, using vocal styles appropriate for particular audiences. Students can also try various approaches to news coverage, including satiric (like Comedy Central or Saturday Night Live) or Stephen Colbert–type reports.

Step 7. Just as all real-life media producers eventually showcase for live and electronic audiences, make certain that their videos are "published" online or showcased at a local, regional, or national event for live audiences. In this way, the student media product is not being done just for the teacher at the school but rather, as in real life, developed for a target audience and subject to that target audience's response.

Assessment and Standards Addressed

On-site teacher feedback forms and peer feedback forms should be designed by the students so they receive explicit audience assessment of their products. In designing these forms, students—guided by teachers—should develop rubrics based on criteria such as project-specific literacy, related content area, and use of media tools.

These rubrics should be continually referenced as the students develop their projects, as well as after project completion when audience feedback should be reviewed by the student producers.

As part of an assessment continuum, the teacher may also want to connect use of electronic text and documents to specific English language arts–constructed response and document-based standardized exam questions.

Common Core State Standards

The DNN program addresses all the Common Core State Standards for ELA in Reading: Literature, *RL*, 1–7, 9–10; Writing, *W*, 1–10; Speaking and Listening, *SL*, 1–6; and Language, *L*, 1–6.

Reading: Literature

Key Ideas and Details

RL.7.1   Cite several pieces of textual evidence to support analysis of what the text says explicitly as well as inferences drawn from the text.

RL.7.2   Determine a theme or central idea of a text and analyze its development over the course of the text; provide an objective summary of the text.

RL.7.3   Analyze how particular elements of a story or drama interact (e.g., how setting shapes the characters or plot).

Craft and Structure

RL.7.4   Determine the meaning of words and phrases as they are used in a text, including figurative and connotative meanings; analyze the impact of rhymes and other repetitions of sounds (e.g., alliteration) on a specific verse or stanza of a poem or section of a story or drama.

RL.7.5   Analyze how a drama's or poem's form or structure (e.g., soliloquy, sonnet) contributes to its meaning.

RL.7.6   Analyze how an author develops and contrasts the points of view of different characters or narrators in a text.

Integration of Knowledge and Ideas

RL.7.7   Compare and contrast a written story, drama, or poem to its audio, filmed, staged, or multimedia version, analyzing the effects of techniques unique to each medium (e.g., lighting, sound, color, or camera focus and angles in a film).

RL.7.9   Compare and contrast a fictional portrayal of a time, place, or character and a historical account of the same period as a means of understanding how authors of fiction use or alter history.

Range of Reading and Level of Text Complexity

RL.7.10 By the end of the year, read and comprehend literature, including stories, dramas, and poems, in the grades 6–8 text complexity band proficiently, with scaffolding as needed at the high end of the range.

Writing

Text Types and Purposes

W.7.1   Write arguments to support claims with clear reasons and relevant evidence.

W.7.2   Write informative/explanatory texts to examine a topic and convey ideas, concepts, and information through the selection, organization, and analysis of relevant content.

W.7.3   Write narratives to develop real or imagined experiences or events using effective technique, relevant descriptive details, and well-structured event sequences.

Production and Distribution of Writing

W.7.4   Produce clear and coherent writing in which the development, organization, and style are appropriate to task, purpose, and audience.

W.7.5   With some guidance and support from peers and adults, develop and strengthen writing as needed by planning, revising, editing, rewriting, or trying a new approach, focusing on how well purpose and audience have been addressed.

W.7.6   Use technology, including the internet, to produce and publish writing and link to and cite sources as well as to interact and collaborate with others, including linking to and citing sources.

Research to Build and Present Knowledge

W.7.7   Conduct short research projects to answer a question, drawing on several sources and generating additional related, focused questions for further research and investigation.

W.7.8   Gather relevant information from multiple print and digital sources, using search terms effectively; assess the credibility and accuracy of each source; and quote or paraphrase the data and conclusions of others while avoiding plagiarism and following a standard format for citation.

W.7.9   Draw evidence from literary or informational texts to support analysis, reflection, and research.

Range of Writing

W.7.10   Write routinely over extended time frames (time for research, reflection, and revision) and shorter time frames (a single sitting or a day or two) for a range of discipline-specific tasks, purposes, and audiences.

Speaking and Listening

Comprehension and Collaboration

SL.7.1   Engage effectively in a range of collaborative discussions (one-on-one, in groups, and teacher-led) with diverse partners on grade 7 topics, texts, and issues, building on others' ideas and expressing their own clearly.

SL.7.2 Analyze the main ideas and supporting details presented in diverse media and formats (e.g., visually, quantitatively, orally) and explain how the ideas clarify a topic, text, or issue under study.

SL.7.3 Delineate a speaker's argument and specific claims, evaluating the soundness of the reasoning and the relevance and sufficiency of the evidence.

Presentation of Knowledge and Ideas

SL.7.4 Present claims and findings, emphasizing salient points in a focused, coherent manner with pertinent descriptions, facts, details, and examples; use appropriate eye contact, adequate volume, and clear pronunciation.

SL.7.5 Include multimedia components and visual displays in presentations to clarify claims and findings and emphasize salient points.

SL.7.6 Adapt speech to a variety of contexts and tasks, demonstrating command of formal English when indicated or appropriate.

Language

Conventions of Standard English

L.7.1 Demonstrate command of the conventions of standard English grammar and usage when writing or speaking.

L.7.2 Demonstrate command of the conventions of standard English capitalization, punctuation, and spelling when writing.

Knowledge of Language

L.7.3 Use knowledge of language and its conventions when writing, speaking, reading, or listening.

Vocabulary Acquisition and Use

L.7.4 Determine or clarify the meaning of unknown and multiple-meaning words and phrases based on *grade 7 reading and content*, choosing flexibly from a range of strategies.

L.7.5 Demonstrate understanding of figurative language, word relationships, and nuances in word meanings.

L.7.6   Acquire and use accurately grade-appropriate general academic and domain-specific words and phrases; gather vocabulary knowledge when considering a word or phrase important to comprehension or expression.

Conclusion: College Readiness and Other Real-World Connections

Beyond its authentication of the Common Core English Language Arts literacy goals, the DNN program validates and concretizes college and career readiness. Indeed, students walk away from this program not only able to demonstrate competence in using technology but also able to use persuasive, argumentative, and informational language as required in the Common Core ELA standards. Further, they can design fully viable television commercials, Power Point presentations, documentary videos, and other media messages. Attaching these electronic products to a resume powerfully demonstrates their competence as participants in the global media marketplace. This practice also affects the real-life citizenship and civics connection for its participants since they have not only investigated issues and challenges, but also taken the time to develop media products that reflect their analysis and studies of these issues. Rather than waiting until they are adults, DNN participants immediately are engaged in social problem investigation.

Here's what Anya, a DNN eighth grader has to say about it:

> I had always pictured myself being a lot of things, but never had I once thought that I could or would dare to be an anchor. It was just something I never thought I could do. Now look at me. I'm writing scripts, coming up with ideas of my own, and helping my partners with their scripts. There is absolutely no way that I could give up doing this. I won't stop my media work now. Watch out for me, or rather tune in to catch me on air!!!

References

Cooper, J. D., & Kiger, N. D. (2003). *Literacy: Helping children construct meaning.* (5th ed.). New York, NY: Houghton Mifflin.

CHAPTER 16

Providing Feedback in the Writing Process with Digital Audio and Video

William L. Bass

LEVEL

Grades K–12 / Ages 5–18 / Elementary, Middle, and High School

TECHNOLOGIES

Vocaroo, Audioboo, Camtasia, Jing, Vimeo

LITERACY

Writing feedback

STANDARDS

ISTE Standards•S, CCSS for ELA (Reading: Informational Text, *RI*; Writing, *W*; Speaking and Listening, *SL*; and Language, *L*)

Thinking back to my early years as an English teacher, I vividly remember my experience in the writing classroom. I spent hours correcting my students' papers and providing feedback at every stage of the writing process. From monitoring prewriting brainstorming to reading their final drafts, I would sit, pen in hand, offering comments, corrections, redirections, and considerations to my students as they were learning the craft. At that point—many years before the modern internet—technology wasn't part of my teaching process or accessible to most of my students.

Times have certainly changed! With digital tools and online spaces to combine traditional and online learning, students are publishing and submitting their work in ways that differ dramatically from the stack of papers that I used to lug home.

Feedback Is Critical

One thing hasn't changed during my teaching career: Meaningful feedback is still of utmost importance, including in our new digital environments. As students learn to write, they need constant, considered feedback to guide them as they revise their work. Many teachers still provide this feedback the old fashioned way: printing out student writing, grabbing a pen or pencil, and marking up papers with editing marks and margin comments. This practice is changing though: By using digital tools and resources, teachers can model the use of technology while providing students from kindergarten through high school (and beyond) feedback in a unique and personal manner.

Audio Feedback

One great new way to give students feedback on their writing is by recording audio comments that would normally be written. The process is relatively easy and can bring great rewards to students by engaging their auditory sense. Two of the most basic and successful digital feedback approaches are embedding an audio file into the text or comment, and linking to an audio recording that is stored online. Each of these methods has its own benefits, and the method should be chosen depending upon the digital environment and availability of student access to the internet.

Embed Feedback In a Document

If internet access is limited for students, it might be best to embed the audio file directly into the student's document. Using this method, students will be able to access a teacher's audio comment whether or not they have internet access. You should note that when audio is added to a document, the file size will grow significantly. Keeping feedback comments short and to the point is the key to keeping file sizes manageable.

If a student submits a paper written in Microsoft Word, recording and embedding an audio file directly into the document is relatively easy using the sound recorder software built into Windows. Record the appropriate feedback, select an appropriate file name, and save it to the computer. Then insert a comment into the text where feedback is needed. For this feedback method, I suggest using the "New Comment" feature on the Review tab so that the paper formatting isn't changed by the audio comment icon. Click on the Insert tab and select "Object." On the Create from File tab, navigate to your audio file and click "OK." You will then see an icon in the comment with the name of the file. Clicking on this icon will launch the default media player to play the feedback for the student. You will find a step-by-step tutorial document for this process at Mr. Bass Online.

For Windows: www.mrbassonline.com/documents/audiofeedback.pdf

In a Mac environment, the process is similar. First, highlight the text that you would like to comment on and click on the Insert dropdown menu. Select "New Comment" to add a comment bubble in the right hand margin and put your cursor inside as if you were going to add text in that comment. Then go back up to the Insert menu and find the "Audio" option and then, in the pop out menu, select "Audio from File." Find the audio file that contains the previously recorded feedback for the student. After selecting that file, a speaker icon will appear in the comment bubble. Clicking on that icon will play the audio file containing your feedback. Detailed instructions for this process are available at Mr. Bass Online.

For Mac: www.mrbassonline.com/documents/audiofeedback-mac.pdf

If there are a number of audio feedback comments in a document, the file size may increase beyond that which can be emailed, so returning papers to students should be a consideration. This could include managing papers through the use of individual flash drives for students, or having an online environment where students can download their papers without worrying about size limits on email attachments. For this purpose, an online course system like Moodle (www.moodle. org) or a shared Dropbox folder (www.dropbox.com) could work well. The key is that students should be able to access a teacher's audio feedback comments whether or not the computer they are working on has access to the internet.

Online Tools for Audio Feedback

Another technique for incorporating audio feedback into a document is through an online audio tool that lets the visitor to the website record and store audio without any special software. When using this technique, there is no need to attach a file to the document, which eliminates the problem with file size. Instead, the audio recording is stored on the website where it was recorded, and users are provided with a link to the audio, allowing students to listen to the feedback from any device that has internet access.

There are many online tools that make this kind of feedback exceptionally easy. My favorite one is a service called Vocaroo (www.vocaroo.com). It's easy to use and there is no registration required. All a teacher needs is a microphone (this could be a built-in laptop microphone) to record the audio. Then, follow the simple instructions on the website. When recording is complete, a link is provided that can be inserted into the comment on the student's paper or linked directly from the corresponding text to the audio recording with no disruption to the page formatting. With only a few clicks and keystrokes, teachers can provide students with feedback specific to their own needs based on their own content.

Because there is no login, if the URL of the recording is lost there is no way to retrieve it. This means that all recordings are stand-alone files with no direct connection to the creator. Additionally, at some point these recordings will simply disappear from the Vocaroo website, making room for new recordings. However, for each Vocaroo recording, students also have the option of downloading the audio feedback to their computer for future reference.

Another resource that I recommend is Audioboo (http://audioboo.fm), which works in a similar way, save two distinct features. First, Audioboo requires teachers to create an account, so all of the recordings are saved and can be accessed again from the account. (Please note, with the free account each recording is limited to three minutes.) Second, Audioboo has both iOS and Android apps, so feedback can be recorded via mobile devices. Once recorded, the provided link must still be pasted into the comments section of a paper, but it does offer more flexibility for teachers.

Using audio recordings for writing feedback is not a new concept. However, it was only recently that tools became available to make it significantly easier to connect with students in this way. Technology has lowered the barrier to entry and given teachers more opportunity to provide timely and meaningful feedback as students work on their revisions.

Video Feedback

Another way to provide feedback is through video. Video files are considerably larger than the audio files, so embedding them is not recommended. When working with video feedback, easy access to internet-enabled devices is almost a necessity, as students must be able to watch the video content easily. Online video is the most efficient means to view and share videos. Sites such as YouTube (www.youtube.com), Vimeo (www.vimeo.com), SchoolTube (www.schooltube.com), and TeacherTube (www.teachertube.com) make sharing videos simple and efficient. Each has its own set of permissions and privacy guidelines.

Two basic feedback techniques are most commonly used: screencasting and video messages. It is important to choose the best method to meet the needs of students. Giving feedback through screencasting requires either a piece of local software or a website that will record. Once the software or website begins recording, all actions that take place on the screen will be made into a video and any audio that the microphone picks up will be added. It's a great feedback tool because it allows teachers to not only talk through their feedback, but also shows students alternative writing strategies.

There are many screencasting tools on the market today, and each of them has its own strengths. My favorite one for longer form feedback (more than five minutes total) is Camtasia Studio developed by TechSmith (www.techsmith.com/camtasia.html). This is not a free program, but provides the ability to zoom in on specific areas of the screen for emphasis and has a great many options for exporting the video, either to be posted online or saved as a file on the computer. Additionally, there are a number of effects and tools that can be used to mark up the paper or the screen.

Camtasia can become somewhat time-consuming as you edit the video. The video needs to be uploaded and stored somewhere online (YouTube, etc.), or the file can be distributed via a flash drive or other portable media, and links will still need to be created using the Comments function of the student's paper. TechSmith also has a free product called Jing (www.techsmith.com/jing.html) that can be used for screencasting. It offers much of the same functionality as Camtasia, but lacks the editing tools to fix video or audio mistakes and limits the recording to five minutes. Once you create a video with Jing, you can upload and share it via TechSmith's servers, making it easy to create and distribute the video.

Other options for screencasting are to use online tools like screenr (www.screenr.com). All screencasts created with screenr are public; make sure to protect the privacy of your students using your school's guidelines. One of the benefits is that when a video is recorded, it is also hosted on the screenr site and a link is provided to share with the student. In addition, the file is available for download from screenr and can be distributed or uploaded as needed. Screenr is a free service although videos are limited to five minutes.

When using screencasting software, teachers should be cognizant of the privacy of their students. I typically suggest Vimeo, as it allows for teachers to password-protect videos. One way around the need for this is to create more generic feedback, such as grammar rules and sentence structure videos, to be posted on a public sharing site, giving teachers a ready-made bank of videos that can address the most common problems found in student writing. This way, student work is not shared publicly, but the teacher can link to a feedback video whenever a student needs help in a specific area.

Video messages are another way to provide video feedback. Using a webcam, teachers can respond to student work in a holistic way, addressing the entire piece. I have found most success using this in conjunction with the scoring guide you used for that assignment. By recording your comments while talking through the scoring rubric with students, your video gives you the opportunity to "speak" with each student. Typically, webcams and modern computers are already equipped with recording software that will save the recording so that it can be uploaded or shared using physical media. Vimeo is an excellent choice because of the optional password protection.

Once you become familiar with these tools and techniques, teach your students how to use them as an option for peer editing.

Standards Addressed

The process of giving feedback through audio and video can help meet the goals and standards for any writing assignment in a variety of ways. Whether your digital feedback project is used by teachers to give students feedback, or by students providing peer feedback, this part of the writing process is crucial to the development of students as writers, and can help to meet the ISTE Standards for Students (ISTE Standards•S), ISTE Standards for Teachers (ISTE Standards•T), and Common Core State Standards in ELA.

ISTE Standards for Students (ISTE Standards•S)

2. **Communication and Collaboration**

    Students use digital media and environments to communicate and work collaboratively, including at a distance, to support individual learning and contribute to the learning of others.

4. **Critical Thinking, Problem Solving, and Decision Making**

    Students use critical-thinking skills to plan and conduct research, manage projects, solve problems, and make informed decisions using appropriate digital tools and resources.

ISTE Standards for Teachers (ISTE Standards•T)

1. **Facilitate and Inspire Student Learning and Creativity**

    Teachers use their knowledge of subject matter, teaching and learning, and technology to facilitate experiences that advance student learning, creativity, and innovation in both face-to-face and virtual environments.

2. **Design and Develop Digital-Age Learning Experiences and Assessments**

    Teachers design, develop, and evaluate authentic learning experiences and assessments incorporating contemporary tools and resources to maximize content learning in context and to develop the knowledge, skills, and attitudes identified in the ISTE Standards•S.

3. **Model Digital-Age Work and Learning**

    Teachers exhibit knowledge, skills, and work processes representative of an innovative professional in a global and digital society.

Common Core State Standards—ELA

Reading: Informational Text (K–5 and 6–12)

Key Ideas and Details

Craft and Structure

Integration of Knowledge and Ideas

Range of Reading and Level of Text Complexity

Writing (K–5 and 6–12)

Text Types and Purposes

Production and Distribution of Writing

Research to Build and Present Writing

Range of Writing

Speaking and Listening (K–5 and 6–12)

Comprehension and Collaboration

Presentation of Knowledge and Ideas

Language (K–5 and 6–12)

Conventions of Standard English

Knowledge of Language

Vocabulary Acquisition and Use

Conclusions

Whether you choose audio or video, using digital media as feedback tools can benefit students in a variety of ways. These tools allow for students to hear their teacher using the same examples, explanations, and encouragements that occur in the classroom, allowing them to make connections and transfer their in-class understanding to their own experiences. Giving feedback this way allows the teacher to address students with a digital medium, something with which students are familiar and comfortable. Incorporating media other than text gives teachers the ability to bring intonation, examples, and more lengthy and specific feedback to students in a voice they recognize. Combining these tools with more traditional text comments can help students make gains in their understanding and differentiate for students with varying needs. These techniques and tools can help to give students quality feedback in a medium that is familiar, timely, and enduring.

Resources

Video Resouces

Audioboo: www.audioboo.fm

Camtasia Studio: www.techsmith.com/camtasia.html

Dropbox: www.dropbox.com

Moodle: www.moodle.org

SchoolTube: www.schooltube.com

Screenr: www.screenr.com

TeacherTube: www.teachertube.com

Vimeo: www.vimeo.com

Vocaroo: www.vocaroo.com

Embedding Audio in Word

PDF Documents

Windows: www.mrbassonline.com/documents/audiofeedback.pdf

Mac: www.mrbassonline.com/documents/audiofeedback-mac.pdf

YouTube Videos

Embedding an audio file—Windows: http://youtu.be/iqd2hDmQoZ8

Recording audio in Word—Windows: http://youtu.be/iGXzBpKxdgk

Embedding an audio file—Mac: http://youtu.be/BmeKoFkqBy4

Recording audio in Word—Mac: http://youtu.be/-P_4R8Uq6q4

Embedding audio using an online recorder: http://youtu.be/sC5lT-tZO0c

Using Online Vocabulary Resources to Improve Pre-College ESL and SAT Literacy Skills

Marina Dodigovic

LEVEL

Grades 10–12 / Ages 15–18 / High School

TECHNOLOGY

Compleat Lexical Tutor

LITERACY

Vocabulary, especially ESL/ELL

STANDARDS

ISTE Standards•S, CCSS for ELA (Anchor Standards)

I n my experience, when students fail to successfully answer reading comprehension questions or deliver a meaningful summary of an assigned reading, vocabulary usually has something to do with the problem. As a literacy instructor, technology specialist, author, and teacher trainer, I have spent considerable time preparing ESL (English as a Second Language) high school students and graduates for American university programs. To broaden my curriculum, I have always been on the lookout for viable solutions, ones that yield results while also appealing to students.

Through classroom observation and surveying of available research (e.g., Nation, 2001), I've focused on vocabulary as an approach to improving literacy skills. The following is a technology-enhanced, vocabulary-focused reading and writing activity I developed for my pre-college students.

The Importance of Vocabulary in Understanding Meaning

Research indicates that readers who do not understand enough of a text's vocabulary are not capable of getting its meaning. This begs the question of how many words are enough to comprehend an average pre-college reading.

Vocabulary Size for Native Speakers vs. ESL Speakers

While it's deemed that native-speaker college students have command of some 20,000 English words or more (Nation, 2001), which enables them to grapple with most academic readings, ESL students may have a considerably smaller vocabulary—sometimes only 1,000–3,000 English words. But at school, these students are expected to read and comprehend the same texts as their native speaker counterparts. This is often impossible, since reading comprehension begins with the understanding of at least 95% of a text's vocabulary.

Academic Word List of Useful Words

The answer to this challenge is not the quantity of the words ESL students should learn, but their quality. Therefore, a literacy teacher must make sure that ESL students know the most useful words, the ones that are used most frequently in academic texts (Schmitt, 2010; Nation, 2001). It has been suggested that keeping up with assigned reading at an English-speaking university would require, in addition to knowing the 2,000 most common words, the knowledge of 570 other, less frequently used, academic words (from the academic word list or AWL; Coxhead, 2000). Therefore, mastering (in meaning, form, context, and function) these 2,570 most useful words (Nation, 2001; Schmitt, 2010) in pre-university English language classes is deemed to empower second language students to succeed at reading tasks in university courses (Coxhead, 2000). To some extent, this can be achieved through incidental learning (i.e., without a conscious effort). However, deliberate effort is necessary to master the most productive words.

Vocabulary Journaling Activity

The activity described here helps students decide which words are better suited for their learning purposes and should therefore be selected for study.

Vocabulary Identification in Context

The journal-writing activity requires students to read a short story and identify the most useful vocabulary using online resources. They journal the selected vocabulary and put it into practice by summarizing the plot from the point of view of one of the characters. The story should be carefully selected to match the level and interests of the students. An authentic, unabridged story is best; however, low English proficiency ESL students could be offered a graded reader. These usually contain simplified classics but have recently been extended to include prose written specifically for an ESL audience. The activity can be repeated with a number of stories over the duration of a term, gradually increasing the level of linguistic complexity or simply making sure to introduce new vocabulary. It does not require a particular classroom setup since all of the online tasks can be assigned as homework.

Online Vocabulary Profiling

Online stories are a convenient choice for both the teacher and the student since it is very easy to examine their vocabulary using a free online vocabulary profiler. The web-based software I use for this purpose is called the Compleat Lexical Tutor (www.lextutor.ca; Cobb, 2004). It classifies every word entered as belonging to one of the three high-frequency word lists devised by Paul Nation (1990) and

Avril Coxhead (2000): the first thousand (K1), the second thousand (K2) and AWL (academic word list). These lists are based on the frequency with which words are found in general and academic texts. K1 words cover approximately 70% of most academic texts, and combined with the K2 list they cover 80%. When K1 and K2 are combined with AWL, 90% coverage of most academic texts is achieved. Given that the reader has to understand a minimum of 95% of a text's vocabulary in order to understand the text itself, mastery of the three lists will bring the learner close to comprehension of most university textbooks or learning materials (Nation, 1990; 2001).

The teacher can copy and paste the text of an online story into the profiler in order to find out whether the story matches the required pre-college vocabulary profile (K1 70%; K2 10%; AWL 10%). For younger ages, the story can be allowed to contain a higher percentage of K1 words, while college-level students could be trusted with more than 10% off-the-list words, which tend to be complex. In order to identify a suitable story, the teacher can use any internet search engine (Google, Yahoo, Bing) with search terms that include either the desired grade level (e.g., "grade 6 reading") or topic (e.g., "science fiction stories"). In this way, the teacher controls both the text topic/genre of the reading and its difficulty level.

Since students will use the profiling software, they should be familiarized with it in the first few classes of the term. This can be done by demonstrating the program using a classroom computer, by showing screenshots of the software on transparencies, or even via printed handouts. In the absence of computers on which the students can have a trial run, students can be given a worksheet with step-by-step instructions. They can then be asked to keep notes of any problems or errors and report them to the teacher in class.

SAT Vocabulary and ESL Vocabulary Growth

This activity can be useful to native speakers of English who need to expand their academic vocabulary when preparing for the SAT. It is also beneficial to those for whom English is not their first language. Through gradual vocabulary growth over the length of a term, this activity can lead to considerable increase in reading effectiveness and the ability to read more and more demanding texts, thus contributing to development in overall literacy skills.

In order to select the most useful vocabulary in this activity, students have the choice of entering the entire text—if available in an electronic format—into the profiler and having all of the words profiled as either K1 (additionally coded blue), K2 (additionally coded green), AWL (additionally coded yellow) or off the list (additionally coded red). This gives the students a wider range of options when selecting the vocabulary they wish to include in their vocabulary journal. Alternatively, the students can enter single words or tentative word lists to get feedback on their usefulness. For SAT prep, AWL words are worthy of learning and off-the-list words are worth looking at. For ESL vocabulary growth, words belonging to K1, K2, or AWL are worth learning. Once the appropriate words have been selected, they are entered into the vocabulary journal (Figure 17.1).

Student Vocabulary Journal

After reading or listening to a new text, write down new words in your vocabulary journal. Here is an example. Are they nouns (n), verbs (v), or adjectives (adj)? What forms do they come in (if it's a verb, is there a past tense or a different past participle form?). Give a definition and an example sentence for each word, using

- **Merriam-Webster Learner's Dictionary:** www.learnersdictionary.com

- **Cambridge Online Dictionaries:** http://dictionary.cambridge.org

Does the new word rhyme with or sound somewhat like a word that you already know? If it does, write that word down under "rhymes with".

Word & spelling(s)	Part of speech (n, v or adj)	Forms e.g., singular & plural	Definition(s)	Example sentence(s)	Idiom(s)	Rhymes with...
Center, centre	n	centers	the middle point or part	There was a large table in the center of the room.	be/take center stage	tender

Figure 17.1 Student vocabulary journal

Vocabulary Journal

The vocabulary journal is structured around the notions of meaning, pronunciation, form, and use. The students are required to identify the appropriate, context-motivated meaning of the word in a free, online learner's English-English dictionary. Cambridge Dictionaries Online (http://dictionary.cambridge.org) supports both British and American Standard English, while Merriam Webster (www.learnersdictionary.com) presents the American version of a learner's dictionary. Both provide simple definitions and pronunciation sound files, in addition to practical examples of use.

The meaning(s) of the word, along with its pronunciation and various forms are entered into the journal followed by one or more examples of use, often from the same dictionary. According to Nation (2008), writing down information about a word helps a student remember it. This entry can be used at a later point to study the word directly. However, to get a better feel for a variety of contexts in which this word can occur, the students are encouraged to take advantage of a free online concordancer, (a program that presents a word in a variety of contexts and sentences). The Compleat Lexical Tutor offers an interactive concordancer, which enables the user to define the exact criteria for context. For example, the user can restrict the search for the verb *look* to the context in which it is followed by the preposition *at*, to prevent the inclusion of the noun *look* or the verb *look* in its other meanings (e.g., *seem, appear*). This activity not only leads to recognition of many possible contexts in which the respective word can be used, but it also enables further encounters with the word, supporting incidental or unplanned learning (Nation, 1990).

Using the Journals in Creating Character Analyses

The students are subsequently required to write a version of the story from the point of view of a character of their choice, using the vocabulary from their journal. This requires them to think critically about the story, interpret it, and use their imagination in order to make sense of the original. Next, they read their text out loud in class and discuss it with their classmates and the teacher, comparing and contrasting their approaches to the same character. This part of the activity is a variety of character analysis. In addition to highlighting different ways of reading and interpreting the original, all of the above leads to cementing of the new vocabulary in the students' memory (Folse, 2006). This, in turn, makes them better equipped readers and writers of subsequent texts (Nation, 1990).

Finally, the teacher corrects the summaries and students are encouraged to publish them online using a blogging resource like Blogger, OverBlog, or Webgarden in an effort to raise their audience awareness.

Blogger: www.blogger.com

OverBlog: http://en.over-blog.com

Webgarden: www.webgarden.com

If the school has a course management system, such as Blackboard, Angel, or Moodle, the final product can be published there as a means of protecting the students from potential security risks. Alternatively, the work can be published in a hardcopy class newsletter and distributed to family and friends.

The Vocabulary Activities as a Whole

Over the duration of a term, the teacher should select increasingly challenging texts that not only introduce new vocabulary, but that also stimulate more analysis and open up possibilities of interpretation. The activity can be conceived of as circular, with each new story leading to repetition of the cycle (Figure 17.2).

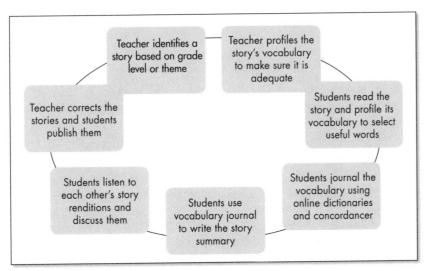

Figure 17.2 Activity flow diagram

Example: From Story Reading to Story Writing

One particular assignment revolved around Mark Twain's story "The £1,000,000 Bank-Note." In this story, a penniless man is given a one-million-pound note while two wealthy donors speculate on his chances of survival.

Here is how the assignment read:

1. Read Mark Twain's story found at www.eastoftheweb.com/short-stories/UBooks/MilPou.shtml.

2. Choose 10 useful words to learn from it (following the instructions below).

3. Using the 10 words of your choice, write a short monologue (250–300 words) that could have been (but was not) delivered by one of the characters in the story.

4. Deliver the monologue in the classroom and let your audience guess which character you are impersonating.

5. Have the teacher correct your monologue and then post it here as a comment.

This is one student's posting:

> Oh my god a £1,000,000 note! Why did I ever let Tod tend to this gentleman. An expert like me should be the one serving him. He must have lots of credit judging by the note in his hand. I'd better select the perfect suit for him. I can't lose a customer that rich. I am sure there was a suit in the rejected clothing pile that would be more proper for a millionaire than this tramp's clothes Tod gave him. Finally there it is. The suit made for the prince.
>
> Perfect it fits him. I should convince him to purchase a couple more suits, maybe some shirts pants, and all sorts of things. The minor customers can wait they won't be paying as much as this gentleman. Better measure him quickly before he changes his mind.

I must be really lucky this guy came in to our tailor-shop. We should do our best to keep him happy with our work so we can get the most out of him. I hope he keeps coming here and purchasing from us. It's men like him that make us rich.

The class guessed that this student chose to impersonate the tailor, who followed the example of other tradespeople by extending a line of credit to the stranger in possession of a £1,000,000 note. Notice how the student is trying to understand and communicate to the audience the greed which motivates the character. I used the vocabulary profiler to check that the student's text contained at least 10 useful academic words (see Figure 17.3). It showed that the words coded yellow were precisely the useful words I expected my students to pick out. The AWL words contained in the student's text (coded yellow on the screen) are *expert, credit, select, rejected, finally, convince, purchase/purchasing, couple, minor*. Most of the words in this text, beginning with "*oh my*," are K1 and are coded blue. About a dozen words are coded green, K2. The K2 word "*suit*" appears three times. There are half a dozen off-the-list words (*Tod, millionaire, tramp, prince, pants, guy*); these are coded red.

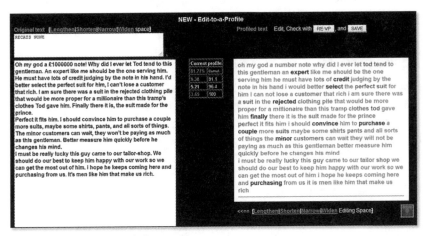

Figure 17.3 Using the vocabulary profiler

For native speakers, 10 AWL words would be conservative. This ESL student met the assignment objectives, both by engaging with the story and its characters and by learning the kind of vocabulary that can significantly improve the reading comprehension of this and subsequent texts.

Additional Writing Activities

In the pre-college ESL group with whom I implemented this activity, I also assigned newsletter production as a term-long project, using one of the five class hours per week. Journalists were invited as guest speakers to talk to the students about writing different types of news stories. The students also learned about conceptualizing, as well as producing, a newsletter. Additionally, they were encouraged to participate in writing competitions. In all of these activities, they were encouraged to make use of the words from their vocabulary journals. Six of my students won writing awards, competing against native and nonnative speakers alike. Some of the competition work was reprinted in their newsletter, available both online and off-line.

Assessment

Because multiple learning outcomes are expected as a consequence of these activities, different methods of both formative (i.e., for learning) and summative (i.e., of learning) assessment can be used.

Formative Assessment

Formative assessment of vocabulary work would include rating the reading-based vocabulary journals for accuracy, completeness, and conformance with the profiling criteria. On the other hand, the associated reading comprehension could include grading the story summary using comprehension criteria.

Summative Assessment

Summative assessment of vocabulary learning could include a vocabulary levels test (e.g., Schmitt, Schmitt, & Clapham, 2001), one version of which is found at www.lextutor.ca/tests, or a language proficiency test which includes lexis. Summative assessment of reading comprehension could be conducted by assigning the task of summarizing an unfamiliar text in class. It must be noted that the above vocabulary levels test (VLT) is at the same time an estimate of potential reading comprehension success, as it predicts to which level a student might be able to understand any text.

TOEFL and SAT Assessments

In one pre-university class comprised of ESL students preparing to take the TOEFL (Test of English as a Foreign Language) and the SAT, the performance of the 12 students on the VLT at the end of the term (Mean = 84.17) was significantly better (t = 4.6595, p = 0.0007) than their performance on an equivalent version of this test at the beginning of the term (Mean = 69.17). In addition, all of them also managed to score the required 85 or higher on the TOEFL iBT (internet-based TOEFL), which is largely based on the construct of academic literacy. With this score, they were all accepted into university programs, thus making this course a 100% success.

Standards Addressed

In addition to being anchored in vocabulary learning research, this activity addresses Common Core English language arts (ELA) Standards (Grades 6–12), in particular the College and Career Readiness (CCR) Anchor Standard for reading, CCRA.R.4 (www.corestandards.org/ELA-Literacy/CCRA/R). The learned vocabulary is designed to help students meet CCRA.R.10.

Common Core State Standards for ELA: Anchor Standards

Reading

Craft and Structure

CCRA.R.4   Interpret words and phrases as they are used in a text, including determining technical, connotative, and figurative meanings, and analyze how specific word choices shape meaning or tone.

Range of Reading and Level of Text Complexity

CCRA.R.10   Read and comprehend complex literary and informational texts independently and proficiently.

ISTE Standards for Students (ISTE Standards•S)

In terms of the ISTE Standards for Students, these activities offer problem solving opportunities, thus leading to critical thinking and the development of higher-order thinking skills.

4. Critical Thinking, Problem Solving, and Decision Making

Students use critical-thinking skills to plan and conduct research, manage projects, solve problems, and make informed decisions using appropriate digital tools and resources.

Conclusion

In a nutshell, my experience with this activity has been overwhelmingly positive. Not only did it contribute to a measurable learning success, but the students seemed to enjoy it, too. What made the activity real for them was the opportunity to use their newly acquired vocabulary toward creating a newsletter, which in turn enabled them to communicate to their friends and families, as well as to the entire community, where their interests lie, what their capabilities are, and who they really are.

References

Cobb, T. (2004). *The compleat lexical tutor* [Online resource]. Retrieved from www.lextutor.ca

Coxhead, A. (2000). The academic word list. *TESOL Quarterly. 34*(2), 213–238.

Folse, K. S. (2006). The effect of type of written exercise on L2 vocabulary retention. *TESOL Quarterly, 40*(2), 273–293.

International Society for Technology in Education (ISTE). (2007). *National educational technology standards for students (NETS·S)* (2nd ed.). Eugene, OR: Author. Retrieved from www.iste.org/standards/nets-for-students

Nation, I. S. P. (1990). *Teaching & learning vocabulary.* Boston, MA: Heinle.

Nation, I. S. P. (2001). *Learning vocabulary in another language.* Cambridge, UK: Cambridge University Press.

Nation, I. S. P. (2008). *Teaching vocabulary: Strategies and techniques.* Boston, MA: Heinle.

National Governors Association Center for Best Practices, Council of Chief State School Officers. (2010). *Common Core State Standards for English language arts & literacy.* Washington, DC: National Governors Association Center for Best Practices. Retrieved from www.corestandards.org/the-standards

Schmitt, N. (2010). *Research vocabulary: A vocabulary research manual.* London, UK: Palgrave Macmillan.

Schmitt, N., Schmitt, D., & Clapham, C. (2001). Developing and exploring the behavior of two new versions of the Vocabulary Levels Test. *Language Testing, 18,* 55–88.

CHAPTER 18

Podcasting
in Foreign Language Class

Salima Smith

LEVEL

Grades 6–8 / Ages 11–14 / Middle School

TECHNOLOGIES

Cell phone with recording capability, Audacity, GarageBand

LITERACY

Foreign language

STANDARDS

New York State Learning Standards for LOTE

The first week of school in French I, students often ask me, "Madame Smith, why do we have to take French?" I try to come up with a witty response that will convince them to value my course. The almighty Proficiency Exam used to serve this purpose, but when it was phased out, I needed something new. I'd like to say, "You should speak another language to communicate in a shrinking world," but I know that to the average sixth grader, this wouldn't make much sense. Fortunately, using technology, I've found ways to make the content of French I enough motivation for my students to learn.

One challenge for any teacher today lies in relating classwork to the digital experiences students have everywhere but in school. How do we compete with all the existing technological bells and whistles that our students use daily, but rarely in their academic lives? We are all consumers of digital media products, but our students—while familiar with social networking, video-sharing websites, and iTunes—are not taught to use their digital preferences to their academic advantage.

Foreign language doesn't get much limelight in American schools. However, it can support ELA literacy when it is well integrated. There's a common skill taught in both foreign language and English language arts: interrogatives. Interrogatives are an essential part of the middle school curriculum. Students are taught to discover the world around them through interrogatives. "What is your name?" "Where do you live?" "How old are you?" This inquiry-type of learning never stops for us; it is a constant at every level of education.

I exploit this essential and enjoyable aspect of language learning through podcasting. A podcast is an audio recording, usually part of a themed series that can be downloaded from a website to a media player, or listened to directly on a computer. Podcasting provides an easy way to reinforce the above skills while giving students a fun and exciting way to learn.

Podcasting en Français!

Who doesn't like a motivated class where the majority of the homework is willingly done and students are eagerly chatting away about their next task? I certainly do! Motivation may have been the main reason behind creating podcasts with my French III class, but what began as a practice I adopted out of necessity, quickly showed itself to be an effective and enjoyable approach to teaching and learning that both the students and I look forward to.

Before we set about creating our own, my students listened to podcasts in class. In order to get their attention and familiarize them with the medium, I began by playing them an interview I recorded with a French friend who was both a journalist and a student. I conducted the interview using basic interrogatives. I played that podcast in class and to my delight the students thoroughly enjoyed it. They listened to and mimicked the way he pronounced certain words, and enjoyed the general vibe of the recording. After observing their enthusiasm, I said, "Oh, you really like this? Great! Let's make our own podcasts!" Their positive response was overwhelming.

The five Ws, (who, what, when. where, why) are an important focus in most foreign language programs as well as in ELA classes. Podcasts provide a wonderful platform for learning the many ways these interrogatives figure in using a language. As an added bonus, podcasts provide students an opportunity to use technology to apply them skillfully and authentically. My French students enjoy leaning another form of technology, and their foreign language learning is enhanced by researching, producing, and performing a podcast in French: language not just studied, but put to use.

In French I, students learn the interrogatives to describe themselves, and this establishes the basic content and structure for the podcasts, in which they reinforce and showcase their learning. One of the positive results of podcasting with interrogatives is the immediate success that struggling students feel when they play their finished podcast.

As their language skills advance, the podcasts my students have created vary in theme from weather reports to the history of French crepes. Students choose these themes, and they are approved by me. Podcasts based on individual student interests are strongly encouraged. No matter how advanced, though, all of our podcasts begin with interviews in which the five Ws are foundational to exploring the podcast themes.

The lengths of my students' podcasts vary. A good starting point for a middle school foreign language class is a minute-long podcast. It has been our experience that a minute is more than enough for a student to adeptly demonstrate the five Ws. However, this is flexible. The length of each recording will depend on the number of students involved. Will it be a collaborative group effort, or will you want to showcase individual student performance? Podcast production is very adaptable and can accommodate both socially oriented students who perform better in groups, and those who prefer to work alone.

As my students became adept at podcasting, it dawned on me that I should have them produce introductory-level podcasts for future students. My students created instructional materials for the next incoming class of French I students. What a great approach this turned out to be for generating school-wide student interest in my French course's activities! Additionally, our school has a strong arts component and the production and performance aspect of student podcasts is appreciated as part of the school culture.

Standards Addressed

Table 18.1 lists the New York State Learning Standards for Languages Other than English (LOTE) (www.p12.nysed.gov/ciai/lote/pub/lotelea.pdf) addressed along with how they are used in podcasting exercises.

Table 18.1 LOTE Standards Addressed and Podcasting Usage

Standard 1—Communication Skills: Modern Languages	
1. Listening and speaking are primary communicative goals in modern language learning. These skills are used for the purposes of socializing, providing and acquiring information, expressing personal feelings and opinions, and getting others to adopt a course of action.	
Checkpoint A	Podcasting usage
Students can: • comprehend language consisting of simple vocabulary and structures in face-to-face conversation with peers and familiar adults • comprehend the main idea of more extended conversations with some unfamiliar vocabulary and structures as well as cognates of English words • call upon repetition, rephrasing, and nonverbal cues to derive or convey meaning from a language other than English • use appropriate strategies to initiate and engage in simple conversations with more fluent or native speakers of the same age group, familiar adults, and providers of common public services.	Students begin French I with simple interrogatives to describe themselves to family, friends, and classmates. Students can communicate who they are to those around them. Students expand their communicative skills from describing themselves to reporting on someone else or a topic.

Table 18.1 Continued

Checkpoint B	Podcasting usage
Students can: • comprehend messages and short conversations when listening to peers, familiar adults, and providers of public services either in face-to-face interactions or on the telephone • understand the main idea and some discrete information in television, radio, or live presentations • initiate and sustain conversations, face-to-face or on the phone, with native-speaking or more fluent individuals • select vocabulary appropriate to a range of topics, employ simple and complex sentences in present, past, and future time frames, and express details and nuances by using appropriate modifiers • exhibit spontaneity in their interactions, particularly when the topic is familiar, but often rely on familiar utterances • use repetition and circumlocution as well as gestures and other nonverbal cues to sustain conversation.	Students begin French I with simple interrogatives to describe themselves to family, friends, and classmates. Students can communicate who they are to those around them. Students inform each other about cultural topics in easy, comprehensible language with ease from television, radio, and videos. Students provide information using a variety of simple to complex sentences with details. Students provide information in the past, present, and future about a topic.

Materials and Resources Needed

Like most schools, ours has a technology lab. For this project, though, I usually use my iPhone's voice memo function. The simplicity of this project lies in the fact that you can use any phone with audio-recording capability, and mobile phones are, well, mobile! There may be instances where you will want to adjust volume levels or do simple content editing on your recording. This can actually be done on the iPhone, or with the free editing software on Audacity (http://audacity. sourceforge.net) once the recording is downloaded to a computer. Another application I use for this type of classroom podcasting is Apple's GarageBand (www.apple. com/ilife/garageband). Students record the podcasts directly in the program and do all the editing in it, as well.

My students work through a series of versions of a podcast before it is considered finished. Students listen to the podcasts in class to make sure they are absolutely happy with their production. In the classroom, with all students listening, I find that the students are able to correct pronunciation errors quickly. Students counsel and praise each other for their hard work. The podcasting production process, from beginning to end, becomes a peer teaching and learning opportunity.

I find that having a website on which to post our audio recordings, one that allows student interaction throughout the unit, is one of my most helpful resources. The easy-to-use websites that I like are Engrade (www.engrade.com), and TeacherEase (www.teacherease.com). Here are some key features of these that support my class in podcasting activities:

- Students can message each other.

- Students can listen to audio files.

- Students can review files and documents the teacher has uploaded.

- I can post homework, freeing up class time for in-class podcast preparation.

My students' performance and learning is assessed by a rubric that I share with them. Student podcasts are evaluated for grammar, content communication, and task completion on a scale of 1 to 4.

Conclusion

The addition of podcasting to my repertoire of teaching approaches has brought me and my students fully into the circle of 21st-century media consumers and producers. I anticipate that this practice will deepen as each successive semester's students tap the previous one's podcasts for information, guidance, and inspiration and build on it as they, too, become podcast producers pushing the French class and podcasting connection further and further.

Resources

Websites

Audacity: www.audacity.com

Engrade: www.engrade.com

GarageBand: www.garageband.com

TeacherEase: www.teacherease.com

YouTube Videos

Using iPhone voice memo:
www.youtube.com/watch?v=1no6nOjuUfA&feature=relmfu

Editing directly in the iPhone:
www.youtube.com/watch?v=sRAZrSIWZes&feature=relmfu

Converting to MP3 and downloading: www.youtube.com/watch?v=Ujz5E2y-S6I

ISTE Standards

ISTE Standards for Students

All K–12 students should be prepared to meet the following standards and performance indicators.

1. **Creativity and Innovation**

   Students demonstrate creative thinking, construct knowledge, and develop innovative products and processes using technology. Students:

   a. apply existing knowledge to generate new ideas, products, or processes

   b. create original works as a means of personal or group expression

   c. use models and simulations to explore complex systems and issues

   d. identify trends and forecast possibilities

2. Communication and Collaboration

Students use digital media and environments to communicate and work collaboratively, including at a distance, to support individual learning and contribute to the learning of others. Students:

- **a.** interact, collaborate, and publish with peers, experts, or others employing a variety of digital environments and media

- **b.** communicate information and ideas effectively to multiple audiences using a variety of media and formats

- **c.** develop cultural understanding and global awareness by engaging with learners of other cultures

- **d.** contribute to project teams to produce original works or solve problems

3. Research and Information Fluency

Students apply digital tools to gather, evaluate, and use information. Students:

- **a.** plan strategies to guide inquiry

- **b.** locate, organize, analyze, evaluate, synthesize, and ethically use information from a variety of sources and media

- **c.** evaluate and select information sources and digital tools based on the appropriateness to specific tasks

- **d.** process data and report results

4. Critical Thinking, Problem Solving, and Decision Making

Students use critical-thinking skills to plan and conduct research, manage projects, solve problems, and make informed decisions using appropriate digital tools and resources. Students:

- **a.** identify and define authentic problems and significant questions for investigation

- **b.** plan and manage activities to develop a solution or complete a project

- **c.** collect and analyze data to identify solutions and make informed decisions

- **d.** use multiple processes and diverse perspectives to explore alternative solutions

5. **Digital Citizenship**

   Students understand human, cultural, and societal issues related to technology and practice legal and ethical behavior. Students:

   a.   advocate and practice the safe, legal, and responsible use of information and technology

   b.   exhibit a positive attitude toward using technology that supports collaboration, learning, and productivity

   c.   demonstrate personal responsibility for lifelong learning

   d.   exhibit leadership for digital citizenship

6. **Technology Operations and Concepts**

   Students demonstrate a sound understanding of technology concepts, systems, and operations. Students:

   a.   understand and use technology systems

   b.   select and use applications effectively and productively

   c.   troubleshoot systems and applications

   d.   transfer current knowledge to the learning of new technologies

ISTE Standards for Teachers

All classroom teachers should be prepared to meet the following standards and performance indicators.

1. **Facilitate and Inspire Student Learning and Creativity**

    Teachers use their knowledge of subject matter, teaching and learning, and technology to facilitate experiences that advance student learning, creativity, and innovation in both face-to-face and virtual environments. Teachers:

    a. promote, support, and model creative and innovative thinking and inventiveness

    b. engage students in exploring real-world issues and solving authentic problems using digital tools and resources

    c. promote student reflection using collaborative tools to reveal and clarify students' conceptual understanding and thinking, planning, and creative processes

    d. model collaborative knowledge construction by engaging in learning with students, colleagues, and others in face-to-face and virtual environments

2. **Design and Develop Digital-Age Learning Experiences and Assessments**

    Teachers design, develop, and evaluate authentic learning experiences and assessments incorporating contemporary tools and resources to maximize content learning in context and to develop the knowledge, skills, and attitudes identified in the ISTE Standards•S. Teachers:

    a. design or adapt relevant learning experiences that incorporate digital tools and resources to promote student learning and creativity

    b. develop technology-enriched learning environments that enable all students to pursue their individual curiosities and become active participants in setting their own educational goals, managing their own learning, and assessing their own progress

    c. customize and personalize learning activities to address students' diverse learning styles, working strategies, and abilities using digital tools and resources

d. provide students with multiple and varied formative and summative assessments aligned with content and technology standards and use resulting data to inform learning and teaching

3. Model Digital-Age Work and Learning

Teachers exhibit knowledge, skills, and work processes representative of an innovative professional in a global and digital society. Teachers:

a. demonstrate fluency in technology systems and the transfer of current knowledge to new technologies and situations

b. collaborate with students, peers, parents, and community members using digital tools and resources to support student success and innovation

c. communicate relevant information and ideas effectively to students, parents, and peers using a variety of digital-age media and formats

d. model and facilitate effective use of current and emerging digital tools to locate, analyze, evaluate, and use information resources to support research and learning

4. Promote and Model Digital Citizenship and Responsibility

Teachers understand local and global societal issues and responsibilities in an evolving digital culture and exhibit legal and ethical behavior in their professional practices. Teachers:

a. advocate, model, and teach safe, legal, and ethical use of digital information and technology, including respect for copyright, intellectual property, and the appropriate documentation of sources

b. address the diverse needs of all learners by using learner-centered strategies and providing equitable access to appropriate digital tools and resources

c. promote and model digital etiquette and responsible social interactions related to the use of technology and information

d. develop and model cultural understanding and global awareness by engaging with colleagues and students of other cultures using digital-age communication and collaboration tools

5.   Engage in Professional Growth and Leadership

Teachers continuously improve their professional practice, model lifelong learning, and exhibit leadership in their school and professional community by promoting and demonstrating the effective use of digital tools and resources. Teachers:

a.   participate in local and global learning communities to explore creative applications of technology to improve student learning

b.   exhibit leadership by demonstrating a vision of technology infusion, participating in shared decision making and community building, and developing the leadership and technology skills of others

c.   evaluate and reflect on current research and professional practice on a regular basis to make effective use of existing and emerging digital tools and resources in support of student learning

d.   contribute to the effectiveness, vitality, and self-renewal of the teaching profession and of their school and community

© 2008 International Society for Technology in Education (ISTE), www.iste.org. All rights reserved.

Index

A

Abumrad, Jad. *See* podcasting to foster speech and debate skills
academic word list, 204–205
activities. *See also specific activities*
    authentic, 5
    by school level, 2–4
American Association of School Librarians (AASL) Standards for the 21st-Century Learner, 7, 8. *See also specific activities*
animations to pitch original short stories, 26–31
    Animoto, 26–28
    assessment, 29
    short story guidelines, 27
    standards addressed, 29–30
    visual literacy, impact of, 31
Animoto
    about, 16
    basics, 17
    book trailers, digital, 16–18
    educator accounts, 26–27
    music, adding, 18
    preparation, 16–17
    rendering final video, 18
    short stories, pitching, 26–28
argumentative essays using Evernote, 138–148, 139–140
    about, 138
    assessment, 147–148
    digital writing workshop, 138
    field work, 144–145
    process, documenting, 141–144
    research, beginning, 140–141
    research, pulling together, 145
    sources, capturing, 141–145
    standards addressed, 146–147
art teachers, 56

Audacity, 175–178, 221
audio feedback on writing, 194–197, 201
Audioboo, 196
authentic activities, 5

B

Baf's Guide to the IF Archive, 105
Blogger, Google's, 165
blogging, 80–87, 163–167. *See also* threaded discussion as persuasive prewriting tool
    assessment, 86
    background, 80–81
    basics, beyond the, 84
    benefits of, 163
    implementing, 81–82, 164
    persuasive writing, teaching/learning through, 153–154
    reflections on, 84–85
    rubrics, 76
    setting up blogs, 83
    standards addressed, 86–87, 165–167
    student voice, honoring through, 80–87
    tools and resources, 164–165
    writers, supporting through, 163–167
Bluford Series, 15
book trailers, digital, 15–24
    about, 15–16
    Animoto for, 16–18
    assessment, 19
    music, adding, 18
    preparation, 16–17
    rendering final video, 18
    rubric for assessing, 19
    sample, 23
    standards addressed, 22
booktalks, 14–15. *See also* book trailers, digital

C

Cambridge Dictionaries Online, 207, 208
camera shots and angles, 36, 45
Camtasia Studio, 197–198
character analyses, vocabulary journals in, 208–209
collaboration, fostering, 167–171
college readiness, 192
comic strips, 112–119
    about, 112–113
    assessment, 117
    ELL and special needs, 116–117
    Shakespeare and performance, 114–116
    standards addressed, 117–119
    technology, 113–114
Common Core State Standards (CCSS), 5–6, 8–10, 139–140. *See also specific activities*
competitions, movie, 49
competitions, writing, 212
Compleat Lexical Tutor, 205–207, 208
concordancers, 208
copyright law, 18, 58
costumes, 48
CoveritLive, 73, 74
Crossing the Wire (Hobbs), 80–82, 84–87

D

debate skills. *See* podcasting to foster speech and debate skills
digital movie projects. *See* moviemaking
Ditmas News Network (DNN). *See* television news production, digital
Do-It-Yourself Digital 3D Storytelling, 54–66
    art, 62
    assessment, 63–64
    background, 54
    designing and planning project, 55–56
    developing story, sketches, and script, 59–62
    images, 58–59, 62
    modifying, 65
    procedures, 57–63
    project dimensions, 55
    resources needed, 56
    sounds, 58, 62
    standards addressed, 64
    success, keys to, 55–56
    time allowance, 55
    words, 57, 62

E

EasyBib, 145
editing, 131
Edmodo, 71–72, 167–171
Edublogs, 152, 154, 157, 159. *See also* threaded discussion as persuasive prewriting tool
elementary grades, activities addressing, 2–4
embedding feedback in document, 195–196, 201
English language learners, 116–117. *See also* vocabulary resources, online
Engrade, 222
Enhancing the Argument (video), 159. *See also* threaded discussion as persuasive prewriting tool
essays. *See* argumentative essays using Evernote; persuasive essay project using Edmodo
Evernote. *See* argumentative essays using Evernote
executive function, 113

F

feedback on writing, 194–201
    audio feedback, 194–197, 201
    benefits of digital media tools, 200–201
    embedding in document, 195–196, 201
    importance of, 194
    online tools for, 196–197
    resources, 201
    standards addressed, 199–200
    video feedback, 197–198, 201
festivals, multimedia, 49
fiction, interactive. *See* interactive fiction

field work, 144–145
foreign language class, podcasting in. *See* podcasting in foreign language class
formative assessment, 212
French, podcasting in, 218–220

G

Goodreads, 14
Google's Blogger, 165
graphic novel-style writing projects, 91–100
    about, 92–93
    applications, 95–96
    publishing, 96–97
    standards addressed, 97–100
    tools and techniques, 93–94
    as writing skills platform, 96–97
graphic organizers/analysis worksheets, 126
gutters. *See* comic strips

H

Hamlet (Shakespeare), 116
high school, activities addressing, 2–4
Hobbs, Will, 80–82, 84–87

I

"I didn't say he ate your sandwich" activity, 57
Inform 7 (software), 105, 107–108
informative speeches. *See* podcasting to foster speech and debate skills
interactive fiction, 102–110
    about, 102–103
    assessment, 109
    implementation, 105–106
    learning with, 103–104
    resources required, 105
    standards addressed, 109–110
    student population, 107
    student work sample, 107–108
    writing, 106–107
Interactive Fiction Archive, 107
Interactive Fiction Competition, 107

interrogatives, 218, 219. *See also* podcasting in foreign language class
iPhones, 221
ISTE Standards for Students (ISTE Standards·S), 7, 8–10. *See also specific activities*

J

Jing, 198

K

Kirkland, Dawn, 175–177
Krulwich, Robert. *See* podcasting to foster speech and debate skills

L

LaRue, Michelle, 167–169
library media center specialists, 56
"Life on the Screen" (Lucas), 31
literacy, defined, 162
literature circles, 72–73, 75
Lucas, George, 31

M

Mac environment, 195
Macbeth (Shakespeare), 116
Make Beliefs Comix, 113–114
meaning, importance of vocabulary in understanding, 204–205
Merriam-Webster Learner's Dictionary, 207, 208
Microsoft Word, 93, 94–95, 195
middle school, activities addressing, 2–4
moviemaking, 42–52
    accessibility, 42
    assessment, 43
    camera shots and angles, 45
    costumes, props, and sets, 48
    difficulty levels, 43
    evaluating and publishing, 49–50
    group versus individual productions, 44
    guidelines, 43

movie competitions and multimedia
festivals, 49
planning, 45
rehearsing, 48
rubrics, 43
scriptwriting, 47–48
shooting, 49
standards addressed, 50–52
storyboarding, 45–46
time limits, 44
topic selection, 44–45
multimedia festivals, 49
music, 18
My Big Campus, 157

N

National Public Radio Radiolab. *See*
podcasting to foster speech and
debate skills
newsletter production, 212
Ning, 72–73

O

"O" activity, 57
"The £1,000,000 Bank-Note" (Twain),
210–211
Othello (Shakespeare), 115–116

P

Parchment, 105
persuasive essay project using Edmodo,
167–171
persuasive writing, threaded discussion as
tool for. *See* threaded discussion as
persuasive prewriting tool
Pixton, 112, 113–114
Plasq's Comic Life, 113–114
podcasting in foreign language class,
218–223
about, 218
in French, 218–220
materials and resources needed, 221–222

resources for, 223
standards addressed, 220–221
podcasting to foster speech and debate
skills, 124–135
about, 124
analyzing and preparing, 126–127
assessment, 131
background of practice, 124–125
hardware and setup resources, 125
introducing assignment, 127–130
NPR Radiolab model, learning from,
134–135
setup, 125–130
standards addressed, 132–134
writing, recording, and editing, 131
PowerPoint, 63
prewriting. *See* threaded discussion as
persuasive prewriting tool
props, 48
publishing, 49–50, 96–97

Q

quick writes, 71–72, 84

R

Radiolab. *See* podcasting to foster speech
and debate skills
reading fluency, 175–178
ReadWriteThink website, 145, 169
rehearsing, 48
research reports, alternative, 95, 96
Romeo and Juliet (Shakespeare), 116
Rubistar, 74–75
rubrics
argumentative essays, 148
blogging, 76
book trailers, digital, 19
Do-It-Yourself Digital 3D Storytelling,
64
literature circles, 75
moviemaking, 43
The 20-Shot Short Story, 39

S

SAT assessment, 213. *See also* vocabulary resources, online
Schulz, Ashleigh, 163–164
screencasting, 197–198
Screenr, 159, 198
scriptwriting, 47–48
sets, in moviemaking, 48
Shakespeare, William, 114–116
short stories. *See* animations to pitch original short stories; *The 20-Shot Short Story*
Simpson, Terri, 171–173
social networking experiences, 70–77
    about, 70–71
    assessment, 74–76
    discussions, real-time, 73–74
    literacy applications, 71–72
    literature circles, 72–73
    standards addressed, 76–77
special needs, students with, 116–117. *See also* English language learners
speech skills. *See* podcasting to foster speech and debate skills
standards addressed, 8–10. *See also specific activities*
storyboarding, 37, 45–46
storytelling. *See* Do-It-Yourself Digital 3D Storytelling
student voice, honoring through blogging, 80–87
summative assessment, 212

T

TADS, 105
TeacherEase, 222
technology coordinators, 56
television news production, digital, 184–192
    about, 184
    assessment, 188
    college readiness and other real-world connections, 192
    equipment needs, 186
    as flexible model, 184

instructional value of, 185–186
    learning craft of, 186–187
    practice primer, 187–188
    standards addressed, 188–192
Thinkquest, 70–71
threaded discussion as persuasive prewriting tool, 152–159
    about, 152
    assessment, 155–157
    background, 152
    online conversations, managing, 154–155
    resources, 159
    standards addressed, 157–158
    teaching and learning persuasive writing through blogging, 153–154
TodaysMeet, 73–74
TOEFL assessment, 213. *See also* vocabulary resources, online
Twain, Mark, 210–211
The 20-Shot Short Story, 34–40
    assessment, 39
    benefits of, 34–35
    camera shots and angles, 36
    filming, 38
    implementation, 35–38
    rationale, written, 38
    screening, 38
    standards addressed, 40
    storyboarding, 37
    tech equipment, 35

V

video adaptation of short stories. *See The 20-Shot Short Story*
video feedback on writing, 197–198, 201
video messages for providing feedback, 198
Vimeo, 198
visual literacy, impact of, 31
vocabulary journaling activity, 205–209
    activity flow, 209
    character analyses, creating, 208–209
    online vocabulary profiling, 205–206

SAT vocabulary and ESL vocabulary
    growth, 206–207
  vocabulary identification in context, 205
  vocabulary journals, 207–209
vocabulary resources, online, 204–214
  about, 204
  academic word list of useful words,
    204–205
  assessment, 212–213
  example, 210–211
  meaning, understanding, 204–205
  standards addressed, 213–214
  vocabulary journaling activity, 205–209
  vocabulary size for native versus ESL
    speakers, 204
  writing activities, additional, 212
Vocaroo, 196
vozMe, 168, 169

W

Web 2.0 tools, 162, 178. *See also specific
    tools*
Wikispaces Classroom, 35, 38
word list, academic, 204–205
Wordle, 171–175
  about, 171–173
  assessment, 173
  resources, 173
  standards addressed, 174–175
writing, feedback on. *See* feedback on
    writing
writing workshop, digital, 138